IVES

Parochial Lives

Roger L Brown

ISBN: 0-86381-770-X

Cover design: Sian Parri .

Published with the aid of the Arts Council of Wales

First published in 2002 by
Gwasg Carreg Gwalch, 12 Iard yr Orsaf, Llanrwst,
Wales LL26 0EH
✆ 01492 642031   ▤ 01492 641502
✉ books@carreg-gwalch.co.uk   website: www.carreg-gwalch.co.uk

In appreciation of the friendship and generosity of
John and Jennifer Platt
Tony and Margaret Harvey
Michael and Jean Wynne-Griffith
Ray and Di Chadwick
on the occasion of a visit to Wicklow, Ireland;
and not forgetting
Gill Watson who cared for Sam the canine,
and Ivor Morris who looked after our home
during our absence.

CONTENTS

Introduction

We are inclined to see the late Victorian Church as living in a golden age. Congregations were strong. Finances were good. Churches seemed to be successful. The truth was far different, as these various essays on the lives of a selected number of Welsh clergy indicate.

The Church in Wales (in reality four dioceses in the province of Canterbury) was facing disestablishment and disendowment. Some felt it had to fight for its very existence. The 1880s was a time of agricultural depression when the income of many clergy, based on the land, fell drastically. It was equally an age of inequalities, when a few clergy received great prizes, but many others faced a hand to mouth existence. Even those clergy whose incomes seemed substantial found that by the time they had paid the expenses of their parishes, especially the stipends of assistant clergy, they were left with an income less than many craftsmen received. The Oxford movement, with its apparent revival of Roman Catholic doctrines and practices, created fear in the hearts of many church people, so that even moderate reforms, such as the reseating of a church, the introduction of an offertory or a surpliced choir, the use of a hymn book or the chanting of the psalms, were bitterly resisted in many parishes.

The so-called mountain areas, especially in south Wales, were being exploited for their mineral wealth. The incumbents of these areas faced an almost impossible task as they strove to build new churches, obtain curates, and find the funds required for church-planting on a hitherto unprecedented scale. Because of the nature of the Church as a legal body, with rights and privileges, church-planting took time and effort, while Nonconformists were up and running years before anything was achieved by the Church. What made the matter infinitely worse was the bilingual nature of the country, requiring in many places a dual system of church life and activity. Equally, there was a division amongst the clergy, unknown to the

English dioceses, namely that between the Welsh *gwerin* clergy and their English counterparts. The first generally lacked any educational advantages due to the poverty of their upbringing; the second group lacked the Welsh language but obtained the richer prizes due to their social and university background. Disraeli spoke of two nations. He could have spoken in the same way about the Welsh Church. It was fondly believed that many of the ills of that Church were due to the Anglo-Welsh bishops and their camp followers, who obtained the best livings and the prestigious offices. As a result of denying the Welsh people their cultural and linguistic inheritance, that people deserted them in shoals for Welsh Nonconformist causes, which respected their language, their fervent desire for loud singing, and good preaching.

These essays look at these issues from a human point of view, as they affected individual clergymen. A number became famous in their lifetime and are still remembered, such as Archdeacon Bevan, Evans of Rhymney and William Walsham How. Others were once famous and are now almost forgotten, such as R. W. Morgan, David Jones of Penmaenmawr or David Parry. A few were obscure even in their lifetime except from a local scale, such as M. Rice Morgan of Llansamlet or Squire of Swansea. In one sense their names were selected at random; but in another they were chosen from a shortlist because sufficient material survived about their lives to justify their inclusion in such a book as this. It is hoped they may serve as a representative selection of the clergy of the Welsh Church, pastors, preachers, evangelicals, tractarians, church defenders, or bishop-baiters; the angry, the sad, the men of worth and substance, as well as the men of spirituality. The truth is they probably are not a representative collection, for there were many others, especially the unsuccessful, who failed to obtain livings of their own but remained curates for the whole of their ministerial careers, or those who fell by the wayside, whose lives were never recorded and are now just names in registers or the various clergy lists. These were men, half forgotten, as R. S. Thomas would put it, whose names are yet recorded on a higher list than our own.

Two organisations are repeatedly mentioned in these various chapters, these being Queen Anne's Bounty and the Ecclesiastical Commissioners. A brief word of explanation is needed about each one.

Queen Anne's Bounty had been founded by the queen of that name in order to collect and distribute the ecclesiastical taxation of tenths and first fruits paid by some but not all of the various parochial incumbents in England and Wales. The tenths was a tax of ten per cent on the net income of the parish, and the first fruits the first year's income, but thankfully for these clergy they were assessed on a schedule of 1535, so that by the nineteenth century these payments did not reflect their original value. These taxes had been imposed by the pope, but after the reformation they had been transferred to the royal exchequer, until Queen Anne, spiritually concerned about receiving 'church' money, returned this income to the Church. The bounty board was required to distribute this money in two ways. Firstly, it could offer a grant of at least £200 against a private gift or augmentation to a parish. Secondly, it distributed the surplus income by a form of ecclesiastical lottery to the poorest livings of the land, starting with those valued at under £10 per annum, but increasing the valuation thereafter as these were assisted. Each 'lot' was of £200, and had to be invested in land, although this ruling was later relaxed. In addition the governors of the Bounty fund were able to lend money by way of mortgage for the building or rebuilding of parsonage houses, for it was realised that one of the main reasons for the non-residence of the clergy was the lack of adequate housing in their parishes. The governors were also prepared to assist parishes held by pluralist incumbents, because once more it was realised that a great deal of this pluralism was caused by inadequate stipends.

The Ecclesiastical Commission had been formed in 1835, by a government concerned about the inequalities within the Church, which had attracted the attention of the popular press as well as of clerical reformers. The commission was empowered to sort out and adjust the revenues and administration of the Church of England. The episcopal revenues were equalised, and the incomes of the capitular bodies, deans and chapters of cathedrals, received drastic attention. Schemes were provided for each body, in many cases reducing the number and/or the income of the individual members, although life interests and existing leases were respected. The surplus income was used to provide for parishes in populous areas, and in particular those in mining communities. The commissioners were prepared to augment the stipends of incumbents in these localities, and provide grants for vicarage houses and towards the stipends of assistant curates. In those parishes where they had taken over either land or tithe property, from either cathedral or episcopal bodies, the commissioners allowed what became known as a 'local claim', by which they acted as good landlords in financially assisting the work of the Church and the care of its clergy.

I express my gratitude to the Secretary General and the Representative Body of the Church in Wales for permitting me the use of the records in their possession (generally those of the Queen Anne's Bounty and Ecclesiastical Commission), and for permission to quote from them. I am equally grateful to the staff of many record offices and libraries for innumerable courtesies and assistance. This applies especially to the National Library of Wales and Lambeth Palace Library. Many others have assisted me in writing this work whose names are far too numerous to mention, but four need to be mentioned, Estelle Blevires, who assisted in the proofing of several chapters, Archdeacon Bill Prichard and Dr Trystan Owain Hughes who read earlier drafts of this book, and my wife Phyllis for her patience and her help with translations. I am most grateful to my publishers for their kindness and efficiency and to the Welsh Books Council for its financial assistance with this publication.

The capitalisation of the word 'church' is always a minefield. I have used the upper case for titles, denominations and the 'Church' as a national or spiritual body, and lower case for a church building and church based activities, such as church planting, church schools or church people.

ABBREVIATIONS

EC	Ecclesiastical Commissioners
CMG	*Cardiff and Merthyr Guardian*
QAB	Queen Anne's Bounty
WM	*Western Mail*

William Latham Bevan: Defender of the Church

Readers of Kilvert's *Diary* will be well aware of the Bevan family of Hay Castle, frequently mentioned in the Diary, though Francis Kilvert was simply a passing and minor figure in the social circles in which the Bevan family moved.[1] But William Latham Bevan's significance is far greater than this slight literary fame, for during his lifetime he was regarded as one of the most important clerical figures within the Church in Wales and as one of its leading defenders against disestablishment.

His father, William Hibbs Bevan, had settled in Breconshire through the second marriage of his mother to Mr Edward Kendall of Llangattock Court near Crickhowell, of which county he served as high sheriff. William Hibbs Bevan married a daughter of Joseph Latham of Beaufort whose sister had married Joseph Bailey, one of the major iron-masters in the country, and who bought the Beaufort Ironworks from Bevan (his brother-in-law) and other partners in 1833 for £45,000. Created a baronet in 1852, Sir Joseph's grandson was ennobled as Lord Glanusk.

William Latham Bevan, who was born in 1821, thus came from a home of wealth and distinction, albeit at a county level. Educated first at Usk, and then as a boarder at Rugby under Dr Arnold, where as a member of the sixth form an unusual request was made to him, namely that he should change houses in order to re-assert authority and discipline in a house where such matters had become slack. Bevan did so with considerable success despite not being an athlete.[2] It was a prelude to subsequent service to the Church. At Balliol College he was a contemporary of Archbishop Temple, but migrated to Magdalene Hall (later Hertford College) on obtaining the influential Lusby Scholarship. Taking a second class honours degree in the school of Literae Humaniores Bevan was later ordained, and then served for a year or so in the busy dockland parish of St Philip, Stepney.

His uncle, the future Sir Joseph Bailey, having turned from industry to the acquisition of land, had purchased the manor of Hay in 1833 (and in 1844 the Castle), and with it the advowson of the parish. When its then incumbent, the pluralist William Bowen, died in 1845, there was nothing more natural to his mind than to keep the living within the family circle by appointing his nephew as the new vicar. Bevan was then 25 years of age and he remained as vicar of Hay for 56 years, retiring in 1902. It was by no means a wealthy living. In an enquiry of 1792, established for the purpose of awarding a grant to the parish, the stipend was valued at £78, comprising one third of the great and lesser tithes let at £50, glebe land let at £5, money invested by Queen Anne's Bounty (QAB) of £20, and the remainder in Easter offerings. By 1832 a parliamentary enquiry indicated a valuation of £140 gross, the tithes having increased to £90 and the QAB money having doubled through that grant of 1792. This was probably the income when Bevan was instituted to the benefice, although it was to rise significantly during his vicarate. Nevertheless Bevan was a wealthy man, and it is said that his wife, a daughter of the Dew family of Whitney Court, together with her daughters, wintered each year at Weymouth and mixed in the best of company there.

A return of the income of the benefice in 1896 revealed that the tithe rent charge had increased to £208.[3] In addition there was a sum of £6 from QAB, but with deductions the net income of the parish was a mere £192. There was no parsonage house, and Bevan, as did some of his predecessors, leased Hay Castle as a rather unusual and stately vicarage. He was well aware, however, that his successors would probably be unable to afford the cost of such a lease or the upkeep of such a house, and in his last days in the parish he endeavored to establish a fund for the purchase of a new vicarage.[4]

An exemplary parish priest, although described as a benevolent autocrat, Bevan was diligent in visiting his parishioners and he paid close attention to the church schools at Hay, raising the attendance to one of the highest in the country. The schoolmaster, carefully chosen, was allowed a 'liberal' salary of £80 per annum, with the result that one of Her Majesty's Inspector considered the school to be 'among the best I have seen in Wales'. He also assisted in the foundation of a British School, established the Hay Literary Institute and a Working Men's Club to keep boys and men out of the public houses, organised a Savings Bank, established one of the first Penny Readings in the country, and had a deep concern about temperance. As chaplain of the Volunteers he was called upon to preach to the men at their camp in Talgarth, but on one occasion discovered the men to be drunk on his arrival. Kilvert mentions this in his diary under the date 23 July 1871, and it may have been the start of Bevan's temperance interest. He also gave to the parish an Infants School, a Parish Hall and the Clocktower.

Bevan's churchmanship was not partisan. It may well be that he imbued the broad churchmanship of his former headmaster, Dr Arnold. His published sermons, a number of which are contained in the biography of him by Canon Gregory Smith, indicate a fairly typical middle-of-the-way Victorian cleric. A sermon to the Volunteers spoke of temperance and the value of good associations. That for the diamond jubilee suggested that the English Empire had been given to the nation by God in order to bring Christianity to Africa and Asia, although in the course of it the evangelical Church Missionary Society received an honorable mention. A memorial sermon to General Gordon commended him for remaining loyal to Christ in the midst of rush and excitement (one can almost feel the measured tones of

Arnold here); and another to Archbishop Benson suggested he died like a soldier on a battlefield; while yet another, to Gladstone, almost compares him to Moses! Bevan, whose political associations must have been with another party, seems to have given in to the spirit of the moment. Keble is quoted in his memorial sermon to the vicar of Llanigon, William Jones Thomas, which was published in 1886 under the title *The Watchfulness of the Heart in the Sleep of Death*. Its title derives from Bevan's suggestion that the dead are still conscious of the human world, especially during the communion service.

A further two sermons, *The Place of Art in Religion* and *The Place of Praise in Worship*, were both preached at St George's Church, Edgbaston and published in Birmingham in 1885. In the second sermon Bevan reminisced about the old time Sunday worship which consisted of 'a monotonous drudge' between the parson and the clerk 'varied only by a dry extract from Tate and Brady, sung to a tune of proportionate dryness . . . ' But now, of course, he continued, our worship is of a different sort and warmth, so as to give a glow to the coming week's work. Such extracts could suggest that Bevan was somewhat influenced by the Oxford Movement, and if this is so he would be typical of many of his generation. Nevertheless he was neither a Tractarian nor a ritualist, and took umbrage when that eccentric pseudo-monk and evangelist, Fr Ignatius, his near neighbour, conducted a mission at Hay in 1878. Bevan spelt out his objections in a leaflet entitled *Father Ignatius at Hay*. Ignatius had, so far as he was aware, no episcopal licence from the bishop to officiate in his parish. He found it totally unacceptable that this unofficial mission to Hay (which Bevan had only discovered was taking place after he had read the bill posters), should conclude with a special celebration of Holy Communion, or that Ignatius should baptise some of *his* converts from the parish. When Ignatius commented that an episcopal licence was merely a matter of 'red-tapism', Bevan retorted that this was a strange comment from one who demanded from his 'inmates . . . implicit obedience'. Though he accepted Ignatius possessed such admirable qualities as fervour, boldness and powers of persuasion, he argued that he seemed to be deficient in judgement and in the discernment of character. Furthermore Bevan was most offended by the homage given to Ignatius by his admirers, and the use to which the funds he had collected would be put.

Bevan was appointed a prebendary of St David's Cathedral in 1876, and three years later became a residential canon – a position he held until he retired from his parish. The normal stipulation of the canonry was that he should reside for three months each year, and this probably gave him the time to research and write his church defence pamphlets. At the age of seventy-four, in 1895, he became archdeacon of Brecon, and he continued in this position after he had resigned his parish in 1901 and to within a year of his death in August 1908. John Owen, his young bishop during the latter part of his time as archdeacon, spoke of his labour of love in the archdeaconry, and 'the invaluable advantage of his example and guidance as Archdeacon'. His experience as archdeacon probably caused Bevan to suggest the sub-division of the large diocese of St David's into three. Significantly when the diocese was sub-divided into two after the disestablishment it was his son, Edward, who became the first bishop of Swansea and Brecon. It has been alleged that Bevan was offered four deaneries, but turned them down in order to remain in Hay. The truth of this is uncertain, but he was recommended by Thomas Thirlwall to Gladstone in 1883 for the archdeanery of St David's, then in the gift of the Prime Minister as he had elevated its previous holder to the bishopric of Llandaff. Thirlwall wrote that his uncle, Bishop Thirlwall of St David's, had a high opinion of Bevan but had had no opportunity of showing it officially. Bishop Owen, just appointed to the diocese of St David's in 1897, wrote to Lord Salisbury as premier regarding the deanery of St David's, which was in Salisbury's gift as the vacancy occurred during the Episcopal vacancy (otherwise it would have been in the bishop's own patronage), requesting the appointment of Bevan. Not only did Owen suggest to Salisbury that age was on Bevan's side (he was 76 years of age though Owen thought he was younger), he also pointed out that he had a fine presence and, an important qualification, namely ample means. But Owen recognised that as Bevan had turned down other elevations offered to him, he would decline this too. But he still wanted Bevan to have the compliment of having such an offer made to him. In the event Salisbury had a prior commitment, and appointed David Howell, archdeacon of Wrexham, to the deanery.

Apart from his church defence work, mentioned below, Bevan wrote various articles in Dr Smith's *Dictionary of the Bible*, an essay on medieval geography based on the Hereford *Mappa Mundi* with Canon Phillpott, and students' manuals on ancient and modern geography. These manuals were published by Murray, and translated into Italian and Japanese, and Gregory Smith suggested that they had made his name well known in those countries. It was even alleged, as G.L. Fairs writes, that Bevan was a friend of the missionary Dr Livingstone, and assisted him in the writing of some of his books.[5]

Writing the preface to Gregory Smith's memorial volume to Bevan, Bishop John Owen wrote, in words that link this biographical section to a study of his polemical writings:

The debt of the Church in Wales to Archdeacon W.L. Bevan is great. He devoted himself throughout a long life with a whole heart to her service. . . . I knew him intimately. I owe more than I can say to his counsel and sympathy. His friend and colleague has referred in his Memoir to the fairness, learning, and accuracy which distinguished his writings in defence of the Church in Wales, and his valuable history of the Diocese of St David's. He taught all of us who had to take part in controversy the power of truth faithfully set forth without exaggeration or bitterness.

The man, however, was greater than his writings. It was no small advantage to the Church in Wales to have in the ranks of her clergy one who would bear comparison with the wisest of the great men who guided the Church of England during the second half of the last century. His wide learning was only less remarkable than the rare clearness of intellect which made his counsel precious.

He gave of his best to the work of the Church in his archdeaconry and in the diocese. His long experience of parochial ministry enabled him to enter into the difficulties of the clergy and his wise sympathy will be long remembered by them. No clergyman in the diocese ever appealed to him in vain for support and counsel in any undertaking.

No one whom I ever met understood so thoroughly the causes of the depression of the Church in Wales in the past, the forces that made for her remarkable revival last century, and the things that are still needed to make her future progress sure. He continued to enter up to the last, with astonishing freshness of sympathy, into every project which made for the advance of the Church. He never lost his hopefulness for her future as he saw the storm gathering round her. His memory deserves indeed, to be held in honour for all that he was and did for the Church in Wales.

Bevan's writings were characterised by a clear and concise style, terse and to the point. He stated his facts clearly and used them logically. Above all, he asked for justice. As he wrote in his 1886 pamphlet on *Welsh Denominational Statistics* the Church in Wales was entitled to common justice, and the Liberationist leaders were not strengthening their course by 'these unworthy attempts to unduly depreciate her in the eyes of the public'. In his pamphlet, *Church Property and the Liberation Society*, Bevan stressed that he was endeavoring to avoid any 'irritating language' (p. 19). Again in his small booklet, *Notes on the Church in Wales*, published in 1905 by SPCK, Bevan pointed out that the Nonconformist conscience was rather one-sided, as it completely ignored the existence of a church conscience. He used the same argument in his sermon on the working of the 1870 Education Act, *Religious Liberty*, of 1872. As a result he was regarded by Bishop A.G. Edwards, the first archbishop of Wales, as one of the major champions of the Church during the disestablishment campaign. As Edwards wrote of him: '[h]e combated with passionless precision the fallacies and falsehoods which in the name of history were broadly circulated. It was notable that the Liberationists left Canon Bevan severely alone. No allusion was ever made by them to his writings. They knew it was useless to do so and held their peace.' Archbishop Benson also commended his work publicly at the Church Congress held at Rhyl.[6]

The sense of dignity and fairness in his writings is all the more impressive when one notes that from time to time Bevan could be extremely sarcastic; possibly he felt he had to sacrifice this more natural approach in the interests of impartiality. We have already noted his remarks about Father Ignatius, but we may also note his letter to John Griffith, rector of Merthyr Tydfil, who proclaimed at a Liberationist Conference at Swansea that the Church in Wales was a failure, and publicly gave his support to the disestablishment campaign. Writing in the *Western Mail* under the pseudonym *Clericus*,[7] Bevan suggested that Griffith should first disestablish himself before taking the Church's money at the same time as he publicly denounced her.[8]

Bevan's viewpoint needs to be noted. He never belonged to the then rising school of nationalists, who wished to emphasise the need for the Welsh Church to be an indigenous Church, in or outside of the province of Canterbury. These people, such as David Jones of Penmaenmawr, Sir Benjamin Hall, Dean Edwards, Dean Howell and Archdeacon John Griffiths, to name but a few of the leading spokesmen, wished to see a far greater stress laid on the Welsh language within the Church and continually spoke of the need for a Welsh-speaking episcopate and clergy. This school suggested that the Church had become an alien church during the eighteenth century due to the Anglo-Welsh episcopate of that time, and some even suggested that this was a deliberate ploy on the part of the English establishment to destroy the Welsh language and nation. The evils of the Church were due, therefore, to this Anglo-Welsh episcopate. It is not surprising that many of the opponents of the Church accepted and magnified these arguments, quoting these writers in their own support.

By contrast, Bevan, although he accepted there was a grain of truth in the Anglo-Welsh argument, never belonged to this school. Rather he felt, as we note later, that the problems of the Church stemmed from its poverty and lack of adequate endowments. His background was that of an Anglicised and border society, and all his traditions and interests were those of the English gentry to which he naturally belonged. Gregory Smith noted that he had only a scholarly knowledge of Welsh, not being able to speak it fluently, though he was able to read a Welsh periodical. In a similar way he had a knowledge of French, German and Dutch. Significantly Smith also noted that '[b]y descent he [Bevan] was Welsh; Welsh to the core in his love for the land of the Cymri. But there was nothing narrow, nothing petty in his patriotism. He grasped the fact that the welfare and happiness of Wales are bound up indissolubly in close fellowship with England. He saw clearly the evil tendency of what would sever ties, which made the two races one. Like his friend, Bishop Basil Jones, he protested, in Gladstone's words on Disestablishment in Wales, against tearing a bleeding limb from a living body'. It is not surprising, therefore, that Bevan had no wish for a distinct ecclesiastical province for Wales, and he felt that a separate Welsh Convocation would not be respected due to the limitations of its membership.[9] In fact

Bevan was deeply concerned that behind the cry for the disestablishment of the Welsh Church lay the desire for Home Rule for Wales, which he believed meant that the agitation stemmed from political rather than religious feelings, and was being used to create animosity against England. Nevertheless he was prepared to recognise there were two classes of Nonconformists, those who were purely religious, and possibly wished for disestablishment in the genuine belief that it would assist the Church, and those who were political dissenters.[10]

Though Bevan had no wish to see an indigenous Church, it would be unfair to suggest that he was against the Welsh language. Although he rejoiced in the extension of the English language into Wales, seeing it, as did many native Welsh people, as the language of business and progress, he yet maintained that Wales was a bilingual nation, and the Church needed to accept that the two languages would co-exist for an indefinite period. It was unfair, he pointed out, that clergy ignored the needs of their Welsh-speaking parishioners in order to accommodate the requirements of the few English families in their parishes, though he also made it clear that because of legislation the bishops were almost powerless to prevent such abuses. They could insist on a Welsh-speaking appointment, but they could not enforce the use of the Welsh language save for a single service on Sunday. Nevertheless the Church had to hold the balance between two languages. It was unfair for her opponents, who did not have this problem, being members of Welsh-speaking denominations, to attack the Church on this score without recognising the difficulties created by this bilingual policy: the requirement, for example, of providing separate accommodation and clergy for both languages, which placed an even greater strain upon the Church's limited resources. But Bevan was sufficiently far-sighted to realise that they too would face the same difficulties with an increase in English-speaking people and the decline of the Welsh language. Then, he argued, they might recognise the difficulties and understand their lack of justice to a Church struggling to provide an equal service to both its Welsh and English-speaking members.[11]

During 1884 the Liberation Society, which actively campaigned for the Church's disestablishment, published in the *British Quarterly Review* its provisional plans for the disestablishment and disendowment of the Church in Wales. In two pamphlets addressed to the inhabitants of Hay, Bevan argued that these proposals for disendowment meant that the Church would lose all the endowments which it had received before 1818, as it was claimed that these had been given *by* the State to the Church, but those endowments given after that date were also to be confiscated as they had been given *to* the State in trust for the Church. The churches would be handed over to parochial boards for the general benefit of the inhabitants, whether churchpeople or not, while the parsonage houses and glebe land would be confiscated, and any monies received from such sources as the Ecclesiastical Commissioners and Queen Anne's Bounty would have to be returned. By such ingenuity, he pointed out, the State could seize the whole of the Church's assets, and the net result would be that the Church would lose its national character and become nothing more than a congregational or gathered church. In a particular study of St Peter's Church, Carmarthen, Bevan coined the expression 'the confiscation of all that is ancient and the disintegration of all that is modern'. But Dissenters too had received state grants, and to confiscate one without the other was hardly in agreement with the rules of ordinary justice.[12]

To those like Henry Richard, who argued that church property had been disposed of by the government to the Church of England at the Reformation, and therefore the State had every right to claim back that property, Bevan replied with an historical argument. It was the same Church throughout, he replied, and to speak of the Church being 'established' meant not that it had been instituted by law, but rather that the law had recognised an existing position. The State, for example, had legislated about 'rent', but this could hardly mean that the State could claim that all rents belonged to it. In fact the Nonconformist bodies were in exactly the same position as the Church in this respect for they too were recognised by law.[13] A study of the endowments of Hay and district showed that the tithes were given by the charter of an individual and not by the State (though these spoils, he pointed out elsewhere, were hardly worth fighting over!). In his pamphlet *Church Property and the Liberation Society*, Bevan indicated his reasons for believing that the landed and tithe property of the Church came from private benefactions and not from the State: there was a lack of uniformity in the size of parishes, which would be untypical of a bureaucracy (a rather Victorian argument); lay patronage was often linked with the ownership of property, and each parish remained a separate legal entity, there being no one legal institution known as 'The Church'. A later study of the glebe lands of the Church convinced Bevan that most of them had been given through the instrumentality of Queen Anne's Bounty rather than being ancient endowments. In Cardiganshire, for example, 8,000 acres had been purchased through this source at a cost of £33,577 over nearly two centuries. These endowments were modern, therefore, and this observation was an important factor at the time of writing, for the then proposals for disestablishment had fixed 1714 as the dividing date, so that all property received before that date would be confiscated, and only that given after that date retained by the Church.[14]

Two of the major reasons given by the Liberationists or disestablishers for the need to disestablish and disendow the Church in Wales was that it had become an alien Church rather than a national Church. Consequently, it was no longer entitled to the privileges of 'establishment'. It has already been noted how Bevan dwelt with the assertion that the Church in Wales was an Anglicising force rather than an indigenous Church. His was an honest answer, even though it may have reinforced the argument that the Church in Wales was more concerned about its connection with the Church of England than about becoming a Welsh and national Church. In his pamphlet, *Is the Church in Wales an Alien Institution: A Reply to Mr Stuart Rendel*, Bevan accused Rendel (then a leading Welsh Liberal MP) of writing in the *Contemporary Review* in such a way as to discredit the Church and to prejudice the English public against it. Although he accepted that the eighteenth century policy of putting Anglo-Welsh bishops into Welsh sees was a bad policy, he claimed it was not a deliberate policy designed to eradicate the Welsh language. He could even suggest it was a necessary policy, as the Welsh sees were so poor that English deaneries needed to be given to the bishops in order to augment their Welsh Episcopal incomes. Rather surprisingly, his suggestion that Welsh-speaking men were not good enough for English deaneries was not taken up by his detractors, though he did add that Welsh men had been preferred to English sees. He absolutely denied that these Anglo-Welsh bishops appointed to parishes in their patronage like-minded men, and thereby practiced nepotism. The only cases he would allow were appointments to sinecure rectories in the diocese of St Asaph, thus taking issue with A.J. Johnes's book on the reasons for dissent in Wales which had almost become a source-book for the Liberationists. More recent research would indicate that Bevan was not entirely correct in these assertions. Bevan also attacked Rendel's statement that only Welsh-speaking people were entitled to be described as Welsh people, and then took the offensive by arguing that most Welsh speakers were eager to take advantage of the benefits of being connected to England. His speech at the Swansea Church Congress of 1879 repeated this historical theme, and to it he added an appendix published at a later date citing further evidence.[15]

The argument that Wales was a nation of Nonconformists and that the Church possessed only a small minority of its people was a major prop to the Liberationists' case that the Church was an alien institution in Wales. Bevan took time and energy to tackle this accusation, recognising its 'catch' argument, namely that any Church progress would have to be made at the expense of Nonconformists. Thus every attempt made by the Liberationists to determine the number of Nonconformists in Wales met with Bevan's counter-response. In 1869 a Mr Skeats argued on the basis of the 1851 religious census that ninety per cent of Wales was Nonconformist in religious persuasion. However, Bevan pointed out that the figures given in that census were based on such incomplete returns that by using the same figures as Skeats he could suggest instead a proportion of three to one. Lewis Ll. Dillwyn's assertion that the church people in Wales made up only one-ninth of the population was re-worked by Bevan who argued that Dillwyn had made a mistake: his figures should have read one-seventh. Using Dillwyn's arguments, Bevan calculated that his figures should indicate that in the diocese of St David's, with a population of one-third the size of Wales, the number of communicants should be 15,625, whereas they numbered 33,560. Baptisms should have numbered 2,375, but were 4,884, and confirmations 1,250 rather than the 2,439 of their actual number. Dillwyn's figures were thus rendered rather suspect, to say the least. Dr Rees was accused of including within his statistics about the strength of Welsh dissent the Welsh Nonconformists living in England, of underestimating the population of Wales, and miscalculating the number of children under four years of age. Furthermore Bevan accused him of having fixed the proportion of 'non-religious' people in Wales at nearly half a million in order to ensure that the number of church people remained at one in seven of the population. Once again Bevan re-did the calculations, and suggested that only seven out of twelve people living in Wales were Nonconformists.

Those who argued that the accommodation or seating in

chapels as compared to that of the churches was another indicator of the strength of Nonconformity were reminded that this spoke more of the weakness of Nonconformity than about the failure of the Church, for chapel splits had made available a far greater seating capacity than was needed and had brought about an accumulative chapel debt of over half a million pounds. In an appendix to his *The Case of the Church in Wales* Bevan pointed out that in a number of Welsh-speaking areas in the diocese of St David's the percentage of communicants to population was the same as in the returns of 1804, reaching as high as 17 per cent in one area. This indicated that the Welsh had no natural antipathy to the Church whatsoever. Writing in 1905 Bevan pointed out that the communicant figures per population for the diocese of Llandaff were higher than those of the similar English dioceses of Durham and Newcastle, and two years later he argued that the same statistic for England and Wales averaged seven per cent, but for Wales it was eight per cent and in the diocese of St David's it was over ten per cent. In his own rural deanery it was seventeen per cent. Nonconformity may have been strong in Wales, but it was not so strong as its adherents maintained, and the Church, far from being as weak as was suggested, was in fact stronger in some ways than the Church of England.[16]

The Church was in the midst of a revival, alleged Bevan. His SPCK pamphlet, *The Past and Present of a Welsh Diocese*, published in 1907, contrasted the position in the diocese of St David's between the eighteenth century and his own day. If the work of Queen Anne's Bounty, the Ecclesiastical Commission and diocesan funds had helped the Church revival, much was also due, Bevan claimed, to the zeal and devotion of the clergy and laity. In his rural deanery, to give one illustration, there had been 16 Sunday services in 1845, the year of his institution to Hay. Now there were 30. Instead of the two resident incumbents out of 12, there were now 12 for the 15 benefices, two being held jointly and only one being an absentee.

Equivalent increases had taken place in the number of parsonages, church schools, church accommodation and free sittings. In other writings Bevan showed how the organisation of the Church and the standard of public worship had improved, and the quality of the corporate life within the Church had risen through diocesan conferences, choral unions, quiet days and clergy chapter meetings. Bevan's pamphlet, *The Church in the South Wales Coalfield*, of 1895, was written in response to Lord Swansea's assertion that the Church was finding it difficult to cope with the increase in population in many parts of Wales because of the difficult legal procedures surrounding the creation of a new parish or the erection of a new parish church. Although Bevan accepted there was some truth in this assertion, he yet pointed out that in the Rhondda Valley and the adjoining coalfield, whose increase in population was only equalled by the Metropolitan area of London, 25 new parishes had been established, 130 buildings erected, and an equivalent number of clergy obtained. Here there had been substantial Church progress in an area of considerable difficulties, and yet the Liberationists wished to withdraw the Church's endowments and so cripple the work of the Church here and elsewhere. Bevan's final and only published charge as archdeacon emphasised this progress, giving detailed figures of the increases in the number of clergy, churches and services between 1831 and 1906 in his archdeaconry. The services had increased from 124 to 280, the clergy from 81 to 122, and the number of places of worship from 124 to 161. It was an impressive achievement, and it is hardly surprising that Bevan was to use increasingly Gladstone's dictum that the Church in Wales was an advancing Church, active, living and rising. Nor was Bevan the first to point out that the attack on the Church came as it was increasing its strength and reviving its work from the state of torpor and debility which had once characterised it.[17]

The Liberation Society had taxed the Church with not

having fulfilled its duty in the eighteenth century. Bevan asked, however, had the Society given any attention to the question as to whether she had the means at her disposal for fulfilling that duty? The Church's means were still insufficient in his own day, but the Church was doing its proper job and was reviving its work. He challenged those who wanted to disestablish the Welsh Church to indicate how it would be benefited by disendowment. If they were unable to do so, he suggested that they should ask in all honesty whether they could continue using these arguments as 'a bait for the disaffected'? His diocesan history of St David's, in the SPCK diocesan history series, a model of its kind, argued that the Church in Wales was always an impoverished Church, and possibly lost out to Nonconformity as it could not provide an adequate preaching and pastoral ministry. It was still an impoverished Church, and disendowment would be 'a shock' that would make the Church 'stagger' for a half century at least, if it did not permanently damage its power for good. But they would not be swayed by the anticipation of a coming evil; rather the progress of the more recent past would inspire the Church with hope and encouragement, and it would seek a still further increase in the quality of its spiritual life. And, as he mentioned in the concluding remarks of his paper at the Swansea Church Congress of 1879, though it was easier to scatter than to gather, he yet longed for the day of reunion.[18]

Much of Bevan's polemical work was written around the mid 1880s when these attacks had started on the Church, and it is noteworthy that many of his pamphlets were produced to set the record straight against the assertions of individuals whom he claimed had grossly exaggerated the Church's position and had unduly depreciated it by persistent misrepresentation. Although the circumstances of the disestablishment campaign changed, as did the arguments, Bevan managed to close down quite a number of false arguments and by his detailed and patient investigation challenged many of the assumptions made. His work as a defender and historian of his Church was incalculable, and however much he may be seen as a shadowy figure in Kilvert's Diary, he was a very real and important personage in the history of the nineteenth century Church in Wales and in its defence against disestablishment.

ENDNOTES

1   D.T.W. Price, 'Kilvert and Breconshire', *Brycheiniog* 19 (1980-1) 50-9; Dafydd Ifans (ed), *The Diary of Francis Kilvert, 1870* (Aberystwyth, 1989), pp. 84f, 90.
2   Bevan remained a loyal member of the school throughout his life, see John Chandos, *Boys Together* (Oxford, 1985), p. 79.
3   The increase was because Bevan had persuaded the QAB to allow part of the money vested in it on behalf of the living to be used for the purchase of some of the tithe income which was in private hands. This purchase, together with the purchase of a smaller portion which he had bought with funds contributed by himself and from a grant awarded by the Tithe Redemption Trust, enabled Bevan to obtain a £500 grant for the parish from the Ecclesiastical Commissioners. This allowed an additional income of £15 per year.
4   Belle Vue House was subsequently purchased as the vicarage of the parish in 1905 for £1,500, of which £600 came from subscriptions and the rest from diocesan funds, QAB and the Ecclesiastical Commissioners. Lord Glanusk appears to have contributed to this sum of £600, although Bishop Owen had hoped he might have purchased the house himself and presented it to the living. Its purchase relieved the incumbents of a house rent in the region of £35 per annum.
5   Gregory Smith, *Memoir: William Latham Bevan* (Hay, 1917) – a work which does not appear to be generally known. It is not recorded by *The Dictionary of Welsh Biography* in its entry on Bevan, nor in Fair's book on Hay. See also G. L. Fairs, *A History of the Hay* (London, 1972), pp. 32, 290-2 [he suggests on p. 75 that Bevan was appointed to Hay by Mrs McNamara, but this may have been a legal fiction as Bailey was about to purchase the advowson]; *Illustrated Church Congress Handbook* (Cardiff, 1889), p. 49; John Toman, *Kilvert: The Homeless Heart* (Logeston, 2001), pp. 193, 339; Fred Grice, *Francis Kilvert and His World* (Horsham, 1982), p. 65-7; John Owen, *Four Aspects of the Mission of the Church: Presidential Address at the St David's Diocesan Conference 1901*, p. 1; *Report of the St David's Diocesan Conference*, 1898, pp. 15f; Price, *Kilvert and Breconshire*, pp. 53f; QAB and EC papers for the parish of Hay deposited with the Representative Body of the Church in Wales. The material about the recommendations made to Gladstone and Salisbury regarding Bevan are found in British Library, Gladstone Papers, Addit MS

44479, fol. 147 (Thomas Thirlwall to Gladstone, 22 January 1883), and Hatfield House, the papers of the 3rd Marquess of Salisbury (John Owen to Salisbury, 8 March 1897).

6   Smith, *Bevan*, pp. ixf: A.G. Edwards, *Memoirs* (London, 1927), pp. 238f: Benson was speaking at the Rhyl Church Congress (*Report*, 1891, p. 39). See also Bevan, *Notes on the Church in* Wales (London, 1905), pp. 63f, and *The Report of the Swansea Church Congress*, 1879, pp. 582f, where Bevan stated that he never accepted any statements at second-hand, but always went to the fountain head. In his sermon on religious liberty (published at Hay in 1872) Bevan argued that liberty should be given to church parents for their children to have Bible readings, religious instruction and prayers in the board schools. To deprive them of this attempt to christianise the nation was in fact a denial of liberty to others, and he regarded this as equivalent to sacrilege. In his *Memorandum on the Report of the Departmental Committee on Intermediate and Higher Education in Wales* (Carmarthen, 1882), he not only defended the endowed grammar schools, which were much criticised by the committee for being sectarian, that is, church based, but also stated his concern about unsectarian teaching.

7   E. E. Owen, *The Early Life of Bishop Owen* (Llandysul, 1958), p. 57. Bevan might also have been the anonymous author of *The Church in Wales, The Liberation Society and the British Quarterly* (London, 1872). This covers much of the same ground and uses similar arguments to those used by Bevan in his later pamphlets.

8   Bevan writing as Clericus, *Letters to Liberationists, reprinted from the* Western Mail (London, 1884), pp. 19-23.

9   Smith, *Bevan*, pp. 3-5, 8: *Report of the St David's Diocesan Conference*, 1898, p. 16.

10 Bevan, *The Past and Future of a Welsh Diocese* (London, 1907), p. 59; Bevan, *Is the Church in Wales an Advancing Church [reprinted from Nye's Illustrated Church Annual]* (London, 1893), p. 8; Bevan, *Church Property and the Liberation Society* (Hay, 1876), p. 19. He was equally concerned that the Liberationists wished to have a 'congregationalist' form of church government, see Clericus, *Letters*, p. 50.

11 *Report of the Cardiff Church Congress*, 1889, pp. 547-53 [being Bevan's paper about the linguistic condition of Wales]; Bevan, *The Case of the Church in Wales* (London, 1886), pp. 13, 33; Bevan, *Is the Church in Wales an Alien Institution? A Reply to Mr Stuart Rendel* (London, nd), pp. 8-11. Bevan also expressed the hope that the Welsh-speaking clergy would be as competent in speaking English as they were in speaking Welsh.

12 Bevan, *What is Meant by Disestablishment?* (Hay, 1885), *To the Inhabitants of Hay: Liberationist Tactics and Arguments* (Hay, 1885), *Church Property and the Liberationist Society, addressed to the Inhabitants of Hay* (Hay, nd), and *Our Parish Church and its Endowments: St Peter's Carmarthen* (Carmarthen, 1884).

13 Clericus, *Letters*, pp. 13f, 35-47; Bevan, *Notes on Mr Miall's Title Deeds of the Church of England* (Hay, nd).

14 Bevan, *Glebe Lands of the Church in Wales, reprinted from the 'National Church'*

(Hay, 1906), and *History of an Ancient Church Endowment* (London, 1899).

15 Bevan, *Is the Church in Wales an Alien Institution?*: see also his speech in *Report of the Swansea Church Congress*, 1879, pp. 358-63, and his pamphlets, *Historical Notes on the Episcopate and Wales: An Appendix to an Address on the Past and Present Position of the Church in Wales* (Hay, 1879), *The Case of the Church in Wales: an Essay* (London, 1886), pp. 63-7, and *The Church in Wales: A Reply to Mr H. Richard's Letter in the 'Daily News'* (London, 1885). In this Bevan claimed that even in the 17th century the episcopate in Wales had not been exclusively Welsh (p. 30), and he ended with the suggestion that Wales could never be a single state because of geographical reasons (p. 38).

16 See Bevan's speeches recorded in *Report of the Rhyl Church Congress*, 1891, pp. 43-8, and *Report of the Swansea Church Congress*, pp. 358-63, in which he pointed out the unfairness of generalising from the weakest area of church life as displayed in the 1851 census; and also his pamphlets, *Exercises on the Religious Statistics of Wales* (London, 1869), *The Case of the Church in Wales*, pp. 16-32, 83-5; *Welsh Denominational Statistics: A Correspondence between Sir Hussey Vivian and Canon Bevan* (Hay, 1886); *Notes on the Church in Wales*, pp. 13, 15f; *The Past and Present of a Welsh Diocese* (London, 1907), p. 51, and Clericus, *Letters*, pp. 7, 24-32.

17 See Bevan's speech in *Report of the Rhyl Church Congress*, pp. 43-8, and his pamphlets, *Past and Present of a Welsh Diocese*, p. 54f; *Notes on the Church in Wales* (London, 1905); *The Church in the South Wales Coalfields* (London, nd); *Is the Church in Wales an Advancing Church?*; *Church Progress in Wales: A Charge to the Clergy and Churchwardens of the Archdeaconry of Brecon* (1907), especially pp. 6f, and his sermon on the laying of the foundation stone of the church of St Gabriel, Swansea, entitled *Church Extension in Swansea* (1888).

18 See Bevan, *Our Parish Church and its Endowments*, p. 7; *Case of the Church in Wales*, pp. 76f; *Diocesan History of St David's* (London, 1888), p. 247, and Clericus, *Letters*, pp. 46f. The clergy, he noted at the Rhyl Church Congress (*Report*, pp. 47f) were often on the horns of a dilemma. As custodians of the parish charities they would be accused of proselytism if they gave assistance to Nonconformists, and of oppression if they failed to do so. He also felt that the Burial Act gave privileges to Nonconformists at the expense of the clergy: *Church Property and the Liberation Society* (Hay, nd), p. 17.

William Evans of Rhymney

It has fallen to the lot of few clergymen to be depicted on a pottery jug. Wesley was one. Another was William Evans, vicar of Rhymney.

Born at Llangeler, Carmarthenshire, in 1823, Evans was the son of a farmer and for some years helped out on the family holding. His family were known to be a godly church-going family, with daily prayers and Bible reading. Wishing to read for Holy Orders, at an older age than most, Evans was greatly helped by the vicar of the parish, the evangelical John Griffith, later of Llandeilo, and the sinecure rector, Alfred Ollivant, then vice-principal of St David's College, Lampeter, who took his summer vacations in the parish where he learnt to speak Welsh. Ollivant helped mould Evans as a theologian by advising his reading, while Griffith taught him 'the sweet and effective ways he had of proclaiming the Gospel'.

In order to prepare for the formidable entrance examination at St David's College, Evans entered the privately-run grammar school at Newquay. He was then a full grown youth and rather out of touch with the majority of his fellow pupils, most of them being rather playful boys. It seems that he was almost self-taught in the classics, so perhaps he attended the school in order to increase his academic confidence. In 1846 Evans entered St David's College, Lampeter, with the chief scholarship of his year, but by that time Ollivant had left for a Cambridge chair, and as the college did not then grant degrees he was ordained as a literate (that is, a non-graduate) by Bishop Thirlwall in 1849. His title was to the parish of Cardigan.

In that same year Ollivant became bishop of Llandaff. He benefited from the work of the Ecclesiastical Commissioners which meant that he was not obliged by poverty to take on other duties in addition to his see. His predecessor had served as dean of St Paul's Cathedral, London. Thus, as the first full-time bishop of the see for many years, Ollivant was able to investigate fully the condition of his diocese. One of its major blackspots was the parish of Gelligaer. This large mountain parish was being rapidly developed by industrialists, with the result that its population had dramatically increased. But its rector, Thomas Stacey, was an absentee. Though he obtained a licence of non-residence from Bishop Copleston with the excuse that the harsh weather of his parish was damaging to his health, it is clear that his background and interests lay in the more aristocratic vale of Glamorgan and its hinterland. As curate to the absentee vicar of St John's, Cardiff, he not only exercised a powerful ministry in that town, but also managed to acquire a power base for himself within the diocese. Although Copleston acquiesced in Stacey's non-residence, his letters contained many strictures upon him and his like. Stacey was required to keep two curates in the parish, but became notorious for paying them the minimum stipend permitted whilst taking from the parish a substantial income from the tithe-rent-charge. It is hardly surprising that the Church languished in that parish while Nonconformity grew.

The curate of the southern part of the parish, containing the parish church, was about to leave, and Ollivant determined to put a good man in his place. He virtually forced Stacey to appoint Evans to this post, at a stipend of £120 per annum and with the use of the rectory house and garden. At that time this was a better income than many incumbents received. T. Jesse Jones, who wrote a biography in Welsh of Evans, recollects that Evans went to see the place and meet his predecessor. There was no answer at the rectory and so he went across to the local inn for a meal. A man was there whom he took to be a gamekeeper, with dogs and a gun and dressed in a red velvet jacket. But he was no gamekeeper. Rather he was the departing curate.

The ministry which Evans gave to this parish was very different from that given by his predecessor. His position was not that of an assistant curate; to all intents and purposes he was its incumbent. If people did not come to the services he would visit them and persuade them to attend, so that his influence grew amongst the people. An evening service was established. The wardens protested at the additional cost. So Evans persuaded people to donate the candles they needed during the winter months! The church building was in ill-repair. The seats were in an equally poor state and more were required for the growing congregation. But the wardens preferred to keep the church rate down and demanded a voluntary rate instead. Blows were nearly exchanged, but Evans stood firm, obtained the bishop's backing, and the new seats were provided.

As a consequence of his ministry the parish's spiritual life was renewed. While his predecessor had spent his days in hunting, fishing and shooting (as Jesse Jones remarked), Evans's daily task was to hunt out sinners and fish for converts. For his own fellowship and spiritual nurturing he walked the eight miles to Rhymney where Lodwick Edwards had established a vigorous evangelical ministry. A communicants' meeting took place here every week, which seems to have been more a seiat in the Welsh Methodist tradition than a traditional Anglican service. Evans was not only greatly helped spiritually by it but he was also encouraged to take part in its proceedings and prayers. It was to be an invaluable experience.

Three years passed at Gelligaer, and then to the surprise of many and against the wishes of Ollivant, Evans accepted the curacy of Troedyraur, in his native county. Jesse Jones suggests this move was connected with his marriage, although it was to his financial disadvantage. Perhaps his bride refused to leave her native county at that time, or he may have felt that three years of hard work in Gelligaer, unassisted, were more than enough and that a change was needed.[1]

Those few years in Troedyraur were probably quiet years, allowing meditation and tranquillity. It did not last long for in 1856 Lodwick Edwards, vicar of Rhymney, died suddenly at the age of fifty-five, and the directors of the Rhymney Ironworks, in whom the patronage lay, placed Evans's name on a shortlist of three, asking Bishop Ollivant to make the final choice. His choice, not unnaturally, fell on Evans. And to Rhymney Evans came, never to depart. Henceforth he would be known throughout Wales as Evans of Rhymney.

****

Speaking at the annual meeting of the evangelical Church Pastoral-Aid Society in 1887, Evans spoke of the position of his own country, and in the following words described the circumstances of many parishes in Wales which were similar to own his parish of Rhymney:

> Fifty years ago you might have traversed some large parishes and have gone up through their valleys and their dingles, and have seen nothing but a farmhouse here and there, or a labourer's cottage, or a shepherd's tent, and you would have heard nothing but the lowing of cattle, the bleating of sheep, and the shepherd's shout. But if you now go up these narrow valleys you will hear the continuous whistle of steam engines, and you will pass from village to village, and from town to town, with teeming thousands of industrious people. Some provision must be made even by the Church of England to meet the spiritual needs of these people who have been brought together from every part of Wales, and even from many counties in England. Another difficulty is the sudden rises in the population. Let a new

colliery be opened, and there will soon spring into existence a number of new dwellings; a thousand, two thousand, three thousand, four thousand people are gathered around, and they call upon us to erect a building – they cannot always worship under an umbrella – and then they must have a pastor to live among them.[2]

An ironworks had been started in the bleak mountainous head valley of the Rhymney river in 1825, and in 1836 a new company, the Rhymney Iron Company, was formed to run these works. Two years later the directors proposed to build a church, provide a school, endow a minister, and build a house for him. They felt a moral and religious responsibility to do this, for they owned the freehold of the whole area and were the employers of all the workers living there. Bishop Copleston was delighted. He had continually urged the industrialists who had brought vast numbers of people together in the industrial areas of his diocese, and benefited from their toil, to act in such a responsible manner. Writing to J. M. Traherne, his chancellor, he mentioned this offer, made in person by one of the directors, and added that they had given 'utterance to some sentiments quite new to the class of persons of which he is now one'. He was later to use their example throughout his diocese, writing 'I shall not easily let go of my hold'; while he included the story of their 'noble example' as an appendix to the printed version of a sermon he had preached at the opening of a new church in Abergavenny. In his Visitation Charge to the Diocese of Llandaff of 1845, the bishop held out their example as one he hoped other industrialists would follow. But it was not such plain sailing as the bishop may have hoped. One shareholder holding ten fifty-pound shares objected that on a matter of principle this decision was outside the remit of an industrial company, however laudable the object might be. The matter was heard in the Vice Chancellor's Court, but the court refused an injunction restraining the company from undertaking this work on the ground that it was in its interests to obtain an honest and industrious labour force. The company had also argued that the provision of these amenities would tend to promote the pecuniary advantages of itself and its shareholders.

A new parish required an Act of Parliament to establish it, and thus a private bill was promoted by the directors which passed in May 1839. It allowed the company to erect and endow a district or parish church which was to be built on a site in the parish of Bedwellty, whose church was five miles away and described as a very small building. Half of its seats were to be available for the use of the poor. The building was costed at £3,200, and its architect was Philip Hardwicke of London. Within a year, however, there was a major depression in the iron trade, and the company found itself in substantial difficulties and, according to papers sent to the Church Building Commissioners, only continued to work the Rhymney undertaking to prevent total destitution falling upon their workmen. The company thus felt unable to use its funds for the provision of a church building. Help was needed from others, so that a subscription fund was established. By 1840 the sum subscribed amounted to £1,300, £200 having been given by the Marquess of Bute and £100 each by the Queen Dowager and Bishop Copleston. An additional £200 appears to have come from the Commissioners for Building New Churches. A considerable proportion of the subscriptions was given by the directors acting in a personal capacity, though it was also known that they had individually contributed large sums of money in order to relieve the social consequences of the depression. They even advanced £1,000 as a loan without interest rather than see the work on the church impeded for lack of funds.

All this meant a long delay before the building was started in 1842, but thereafter progress was rapid, and the church was consecrated on 14 July 1843, not without some problems, and at a total cost of £4,663. Even at that cost its style was spartan, almost industrial, for there was no chancel and the altar was placed at the west end for reasons of space. But the debt still remained and became a source of continuing concern to the directors. Writing to the commissioners on 22 December 1843 one of the directors, W.S. Copeland, MP, asked if they could make a grant to help liquidate the debt, even though he accepted it was contrary to their rules and regulations as the church had been consecrated. One problem was that the patronage was vested in the board of their company (though the bishop was given the first nomination), which meant it was in private and not public hands. The directors had been advised that it would require an act of parliament to place the patronage into the hands of the bishop of Llandaff, but they hoped that a clause to this effect could be inserted into the current church building bill then going through parliament. If this bill passed it was anticipated that the commissioners would then be in a position to give their assistance. The directors had already paid £2,500 of the cost of the building and provided a stipend of £150 per annum for the minister together with a free house, paddock and coals, as well as establishing schools in the parish. By 1849 the patronage was in the hands of the bishop according to the *Clergy List* of that year, but it is not known if this was because the appeal was successful.

A Cardiganshire man, Lodwick Edwards, had been appointed the first vicar by Bishop Copleston in 1843. It is said that church work in the area had already started before his appointment as lay people had organised services and Sunday schools in local houses and later at the Rhymney Inn. Writing to the commissioners on the 1 March 1844 Edwards wrote that since the opening of the church the cause had prospered 'beyond the most sanguine expectations of its warmest supporters'. He had 200 and more communicants and a Sunday school of over 500 (this was probably an all age one). When he had arrived in the parish there were only five church-going families and all the rest were dissenters, but his congregation now equalled those of four of their chapels put together. This remarkable achievement was meant to impress the commissioners, and one hopes it did, for Edwards went on to point out that while the directors of the company had added an additional £50 to his £100 stipend, he had no claim on this additional sum. With a wife and six children to support and without any other means of his own Edwards accordingly asked if the commissioners could assist him. Alas, they could not, even though a local commission was appointed to review his application. It noted his additional income of £8 in surplice fees, but pointed out that he had no claim to the pew rents of the church which, it was hinted, were not collected in any case. The rectorial tithes belonged to Sir Charles Morgan, who does not appear to have been a subscriber to the building fund.

The parish features, although not named, in the Church Pastoral-Aid Society's annual report for 1845. Its description of a district of 8,000 souls, severed from its mother parish which was 17 miles by 6 in size, and with a church built by the masters of the local factory and consecrated in 1843, obviously refers to Rhymney. The incumbent, who had obtained a curate's grant from the society, wrote that without this assistance he could not have performed his arduous duties in that parish. He had 253 communicants and a Sunday school considered the largest in Wales. It was so large they had to use the church for this purpose, as there was no other building capable of holding the 650-700 who attended. There was a separate Welsh Sunday school held during the morning in a hired room. Although he had a curate the duties were heavy, especially as the sick were numerous in these manufacturing districts, and his only free night was Saturday.[3]

'That good man, Lodwick Edwards,' wrote Copleston to Traherne, 'has within one year got two hundred communicants,' and now had about five hundred people preparing for confirmation, adding '[y]et he is "passing rich" with one hundred per year'. Nothing had pleased him more on his current confirmation circuit than the state of Rhymney

Church. Indeed, at a time when men thought the Church was in decline the situation at Rhymney was a success story *par excellence*. As Islwyn Jenkins writes Edwards was known for the definiteness of his doctrinal teaching, the practical application of his sermons, his pastoral care, and for his communicants' meeting, held every Monday night. He left on his death, he continued, a trained congregation of active and instructed men and women whose life of prayer and sacraments and Bible reading made a real impression on the community. Furthermore he was active in the local cultural scene, presiding, for example, at an eisteddfod in December 1849. His early death in 1856 left a huge void in the community, diocese and especially within the Church at Rhymney. Many must have seen his ministry (although it is doubtful if he did) as a means of extending the social influence of the Church into what had been a distinctly disruptive community, known for its Scotch cattle and Chartist disorders, and dominated by the Company with its illegal but nevertheless dominant truck shop. After all, one of the main means of selling the Llandaff Diocesan Church Extension Fund to the wealthy of the diocese was the hope that by providing clergy and churches in such lawless and frontier communities as Rhymney the Church might act as a sort of moral police force upon the disorderly lower classes. But as E.T. Davies suggests, part of the reason for Edwards's success was that the Church had planted itself into the community before Nonconformity had taken complete possession. It was normally the other way round.[4]

****

William Evans so naturally and admirably filled Edwards's place within the parish, and later within the diocese, that it is easy to forget that he built on foundations which had been well laid by his predecessor. Nor was he a stranger to the community, for as we have seen, he had attended those

Monday night communicant classes held by Edwards where it is clear that his contribution was much valued. Evans was also sufficiently astute to refuse to live in the house provided for the vicar by the company, and thus to be seen by them as just another employee. For in his parish, as Jesse Jones remarked, the manager of the iron works ruled like a king. Instead he made his home at Nant Llesg, half a mile from his church but on the Glamorgan side of the river, and thus within the parish of Gelligaer. Here he was to live surrounded by the remains of industrial dereliction, although when he moved there it was with the expectation of living in the country.[5]

As pastor, evangelist and preacher, Evans built on the legacy left by Edwards. He regarded home visiting as the mainspring of his work, and in his evangelical tradition this meant far more than pleasantries about the weather. By 1897 his communicant roll numbered 750, and included a considerable number of men and boys who were regular communicants. The weekly communicants' meeting was the key to much of his spiritual work, as was the existence of 187 lay helpers, who served as Sunday school teachers, tract distributors and district visitors. Indeed, Evans believed that everyone in his congregation should be given some work to do. St Matthew's Church had been built for the English-speaking population in 1880, and there was also a Welsh mission-room, while the services at the parish church of St David's were in both languages. Each church had a Sunday school which was an all-age one for children and adults. These figures were given by the writer of a report about the parish in the Church Pastoral-Aid Society's magazine, and the writer concluded that the spiritual life and witness of this parish was an emphatic refutation of the Liberationists' or disestablishers' claim that the Church was alien and deserted. The parish of Rhymney, he concluded, would not fear comparison with many English parishes.[6] The Sunday School, alleged Jesse Jones, became the 'glory' of church life in that parish, while Lady Llanover told Gladstone that

Evans had the largest congregation of any parish in the diocese of Llandaff.[7] Evans' successor in the living, Daniel Fisher, was able to inform a royal commission within a few years of Evans's death of the activities and work of his parish; its 844 communicants, the communicants' meeting, temperance society and Band of Hope, the Bible classes for men, women and youngsters, the Children's Bible School and the cottage prayer meetings. Many of these activities had been established by Evans during the years of his ministry.[8]

That royal commission also discovered one other thing about church life in Rhymney. Try as they could its Nonconformist members were unable to find any evidence that the Welsh language had been neglected in that parish. The Welsh people, Evans believed, had equal claims with the English people, even though in the past their claims had been shamefully neglected. In fact his Welsh congregation was more than equal to any of the Nonconformist chapels in his parish, showing that he practised what he preached. Evans made his position clear at the 1887 meeting of the Llandaff Diocesan Conference when a debate took place as to 'The best mode of meeting the Bi-lingual Difficulty'. During the course of the debate Evans argued that the Welsh-speaking people felt ignored by the Church even though there was plenty of proof of the existence of the language within Nonconformity! The Welsh had often been forced out of their parish churches and required to worship in inconvenient schoolrooms. In such places the Church could never grow, nor could any reverence be taught. Hence the Welsh went elsewhere. They did so also because they were given the most inconvenient times for worship, generally during the Sunday afternoon, while the incumbent, although the chief shepherd of the parish, generally neglected them and instead sent along his curates to minister to them. It would be better to have two services in the morning, one in each language, he argued, than to retain a Welsh afternoon service, though this still left a difficulty about an evening service.

Bilingual services did not work. What was needed was a dual machinery of separate churches and clergy for the two congregations, though this could not be realised in most parishes because of a lack of funds. It was important, however, that even if the ideal could not be obtained each section should receive equal privileges. Evans endeavoured to do this in his parish, and he believed he had got the balance right as both sections said that he gave all his attention to the other group! Nevertheless Jesse Jones remarked that Evans preferred the Welsh language, and would be at the Welsh service if the times of two services clashed, though he would not allow the Welsh language to stand between him and the work of his parish.[9]

There were other factors which helped to build up his parish, besides Evans's pastoral care, house to house visiting, and the equal provision given to both languages. One was his preaching ability. Though he never underestimated the sacraments, wrote Jesse Jones, Evans believed that preaching was one of the most important tasks of the ministry. To him the pulpit was a consecrated place, and apart from the Sunday services, there were four preaching services during the week. Although his sermons were practical, plain, simple and direct, rather than dramatic, he was frequently called upon to preach at other places, and at times undertook preaching tours of Wales, which made his name as well known outside the diocese of Llandaff as within it. Another wrote about the pure and living gospel which flowed out of his lips, his tender voice, and his sweet and powerful words.[10]

Another factor was the strong commitment invested by Evans and his parish in the life of the community. Meetings for entertainment were combined with occasions for instruction, and penny readings introduced (sometimes attracting an audience of 300 and more). At St Matthew's Church Evans chaired a celebrated weekly meeting called to discuss a pre-arranged subject, religious or secular, and open to all. Starting with prayer and praise, Evans expected all those who attended to have made themselves familiar with the topic under discussion and would call on men to speak without warning. Then he would sum up the discussion at the end. Many said he did this better than any judge, and never introduced his own personal views.[11]

A further and perhaps more important reason for this parochial success was that Evans believed in missions: missions to revive the churchfolk to new zeal and missions to bring in new converts. During the 1880s the situation within the Welsh Church was becoming critical. The threat of disestablishment, the tithe disputes which crippled clergy financially, the over-expectations of parishioners and bishops alike, the hard task of building up new parishes, meant that the morale of many of the clergy was extremely low. Archbishop Benson of Canterbury, aware of the position, took counsel with the Welsh bishops and then with a number of Welsh clergy who were summoned to Llandaff. Jesse Jones told the Llandaff Diocesan Conference of 1911 what had happened at this meeting. The archbishop asked Evans what he would do in this crisis. He replied, characteristically but humbly, 'The Church is the ship of Jesus Christ. Let us remember that he is on board and let us also steer our course straight to the haven where we would be'. One wonders what Benson made of this, but he certainly promoted the mission movement in Wales, sending his own Tait missioner, Joseph Cullin, to head the work and encouraging him to obtain and train missioners from both Wales and England.

It is hardly surprising that Rhymney should have become one of the centres of this mission work. A preliminary mission was held in April 1886. Cullin was later to give a most enthusiastic account to the archbishop about it. The mission had created a great interest. The congregations were large, even overflowing, and over 400 people had come to the first Sunday communion service, which he thought exceptional in a working class parish. The whole congregation remained for the first after-meeting, and many for the second. These meetings took the form of devotions, prayers and self examination. Many, especially men, had remained behind to ask him for help with personal difficulties. Over 1,000 people were present at the concluding service, many accepting a mission-card, while the church people requested a special address for communicants and confirmees. On the day he left, the works supplied him with a special locomotive to take him to his train connection, the works manager begging him to come again, and many people taking the opportunity to say thank-you and farewell. Sixty-one people, he reported, had given their names to the vicar as desirous to receive communion, many of whom had lapsed and some were unconfirmed. New Bible classes had been started for these people, and on Easter day there were 514 communicants, a surprising number, said Evans, whose heart was 'brimful with gratitude', as it was not a favourable day as many were away on holiday.

Another mission visit took place in that October. At one evening meeting over 900 people were present in spite of heavy rain, many of them Welsh-speakers, although most were able to understand some English. About 600 people, including 35 clergymen, attended a conference on mission work held in connection with this mission, while 200 people attended another meeting for church workers. A year later Cullin revisited the parish and reported that once again large numbers of people of all denominations had flocked to hear him, greeting the missioners warmly, while he noted the 'very striking feature' of the all-age Sunday schools. Nine hundred of their members, adults included, 'with quiet earnest attention submitted themselves to be catechised', and they also recited large portions of scripture. Quiet days were also held for church workers and clergy on this occasion. The missioners later expressed amazement at the people's desire for and appreciation of solid doctrinal teaching. Some areas, they thought, were equal to and probably exceeded the spiritual fervour of the more favoured districts they had visited in England. Although this was a general comment, it must have been applicable to Rhymney for Cullin wrote that it was one of the best worked parishes in south Wales. Although Evans was concerned at the lack of Welsh-speaking missioners, a position later remedied, he clearly felt that these missions helped develop the spiritual life which was so wanting within the Welsh Church in general. But clearly the missions consolidated Evans's work in his parish and brought in not only new converts but also a large number of spiritually-minded 'church-workers'.[12]

Throughout these years Evans's income remained comparatively small. There was the £150 endowment from the company; fees of £57 (in later years these were much diminished through the opening of a cemetery by the local Burial Board as the churchyard was full), and a grant of £145 given in 1865 by the Ecclesiastical Commissioners on account of the population of the parish in order to increase its income to £300. Evans had two curates in 1868, for which the commissioners allowed him two grants of £60 each. One grant equalled half the stipend. The two other halves were made up from a CPAS grant and subscriptions.[13]

It is not surprising that ecclesiastical honours came Evans's way. Appointed a prebendary of Llandaff Cathedral in 1878, and an examining chaplain by Bishop Lewis, he was also elected as one of the clerical representatives to the Lower House of Convocation (the Church's Parliament) by his fellow clergy. Ollivant made him his confidant, it appears, and used him as a mediator, unfortunately unsuccessfully, in the dispute between Lord Llanover and John Griffith, vicar of Mynddislwyn, regarding the chapel built in the parish at Abercarn by the Llanover family. It probably helped that Evans was a trusted member of the Llanover circle. Lady Llanover, who regarded herself as the arbitrator of all things Welsh, especially in the Church, even recommended him to Gladstone (the prime minister) for the bishopric of Llandaff in 1882, along with David Howell of Wrexham and Chancellor Phillips of Aberystwyth. Gladstone, having sifted their claims and made enquiries from other advisors, was sufficiently impressed to place Evans's name on a shortlist of candidates, which also included the names of Griffith Arthur Jones of St Mary's Cardiff and David Williams of Llanelli. He later wrote that while they were all Welshmen and men of merit he felt a shortlist of three was too small.[14] In the event the appointment went to the relatively unknown Archdeacon Richard Lewis. Perhaps Gladstone was impressed by Evans's good relationships with dissent, the considerable number of ordinands who came from his parish, and his reputation as a trainer of clergy. One of his curates, David Edmondes Owen, who came from the sheltered walls of St David's College to the 'whirlpool of industrial life' in Rhymney, remembered Evans's dictum to the end of his days about the need to mend one's own nets if one was to 'look in hope for the miraculous draught of fish'.[15] Gladstone may also have been aware of Evans's editorship of a Church in Wales periodical, Y Cyfaill Eglwysig or the Church Friend. David Howell started this monthly periodical, but Evans took it over and continued as editor for 29 years until ill-health forced him to relinquish this task in 1894. It was one of the few church publications to survive intact for a fairly long period of time. The Llandaff Diocesan Conference of that year, passing a vote of sympathy upon the illness of this 'kind hearted, good man', heard Thomas Theophilus of Tredegar speak thus of the magazine and its editor:

I think it was quite right, on the part of one of the speakers, to say of Canon Evans that at the present moment there is no one in the Principality who has done more for the Church press than he. He has done it quietly, unostentatiously, but very effectively. The little Cyfaill is a little magazine which is quite the thing in teaching for the ordinary Welsh reader.

That is a matter of great importance. And then, again, it gives instruction on various general matters as well as Church questions, and at the close of the *Cyfaill* each month there is an epitome of the Church work, not only in Wales, but in the English Dioceses too.

He was one of a small band of men, added Jesse Jones in his biography, who helped save the Welsh Church press from extinction, and under his chairmanship the church newspaper *Y Llan* was revived.[16]

An advocate of foreign mission, Evans not only encouraged local branches in his parish, he also loved to attend their May meetings in London. It seems that the Church Pastoral-Aid Society was closest to his heart, however, for he was deeply grateful for its support to his own parish and to Wales in general. Speaking at its 1887 annual meeting Evans wondered what the condition of his Church might have been without the support of this society. '[Y]ou have the satisfaction of knowing that you are helping, not a dying Church, nor a decaying Church, but a living, a reviving, a rising Church,' he told its members. He continued his theme with these words: '[w]e are trying to occupy fresh positions, we are trying to strengthen our weak places, we are trying to light dark spots, and we are doing our best to gather the people into our Churches.' And though the Church was assailed by adversaries he yet hoped that the society might continue its noble help to Wales 'in order that that Church may do her spiritual work more thoroughly, more earnestly, more prayerfully, and more successfully than ever, leaving the consequences in the hands of God'.[17]

His parochial labours took place in the midst of tragedy. His wife became an alcoholic, possibly because three of her four children died in infancy while their son failed to live up to his early promise. There was no way of hiding his wife's condition: she died aged forty-eight in 1868. The previous year a trusted family maid was murdered and the subsequent trial and acquittal of her boyfriend made national headlines. Evans saw his catechising and teaching work in the schools lost when a local School Board came and took them over, with the consent of the Company, though he became an elected member of that board. But his life remained a quiet devoted one in spite of these misfortunes and the pressures of his parish. Jesse Jones states that he got up at nine each morning, had a time of quiet prayer before breakfast, then read the Scriptures with a commentary at his side for an hour, answered his letters and read the newspaper. At 11.30 a.m. he visited his parishioners until lunch at 2.00 p.m., after which he prepared for his evening meetings and did some more visiting. It is said that when he entered a house and put his silk hat on the dresser people knew it was a sign he would like a cup of tea. Returning home from the evening meetings he read until he retired to bed at 3.00 a.m. This love of order was characteristic of him, wrote an obituarist, adding that punctuality was one of the most notable features of his life.

In 1894 Evans developed palsy, and although he continued in the parish as vicar, employing an additional curate as his own expense, his visits had to be curtailed and his speech became badly affected. Shilton Evans, one of the ordinands from the parish, remembered that at this time he would often place his walking stick on the head of young children as an expression of affection, but because of his bodily affliction the stick was apt to come down with an unintentional sharpness! The end of his sufferings came in August 1900, and it was said at his funeral that people had never seen so many surpliced clergymen before. He had been offered other benefices by his own and by other bishops, but preferred to remain in Rhymney near the grave of his wife.[18]

'No lambs, no sheep,' he is quoted as saying, 'and remember that human beings, church members even, are better weighed than counted.'[19] Not only did Evans build up a parish, though its foundations had been well prepared by his predecessor, he also enabled the whole Church to learn from his example. The battle he fought was for the spiritual life of his Church, rather than for retaining at all costs its position as an Established Church, which was the position of Bishop Edwards of St Asaph and his group. And that battle could only be won, he believed, in the hearts and minds of people, rather than through institutions and buildings. By encouraging lay involvement, and by being fully involved in the cultural life of his community, Evans made his parish a spiritual force in both the diocese and in the wider community. A man of the times, he yet responded to the needs of his day in the name and with the resources of the Gospel. Let the most celebrated of Rhymney men, Thomas Jones, CH, have the last word. '[M]en like Canon Evans,' he wrote, were men 'of great vigour and public spirit – honest, generous, and sensitive. Compared with them, most of us to-day are idlers in the vineyard.'[20]

ENDNOTES

1 Much of the background for this article is derived from the biography written in Welsh by T. Jesse Jones of Gelligaer, *William Evans, Rhymney* (Lampeter, nd), and see especially pp. 1-27. There was also another curate in the parish of Gelligaer who served the top end of the parish from Brithdir chapel.
2 *Church Pastoral-Aid Society, Abstract of Report 1887*, p 24.
3 Islwyn Jenkins, "The Church in Industrial Rhymney 1800-55", *Journal of the Historical Society of the Church in Wales*, XVI (1966) 77-87; E. E. Edwards, *Echoes of Rhymney* (Risca, 1974), pp. 24f, 63f; *Church Pastoral-Aid Society Report for 1845*, pp. 39f; *Ecclesiastical Gazette*, April 1839, pp. 184-6; Edward Copleston, *Charge to the Clergy of the Diocese of Llandaff*, 1845, pp. 28-30; Papers of the Church Building Commission contained within the papers of the Ecclesiastical Commission for the parish of Rhymney, held by the Representative Body of the Church in Wales; Copleston Correspondence, in the archives of Llandaff Cathedral, letters to J M Traherne, nos. 67 (24 January 1839) and 73. (14 October 1839) and to W B Knight, no. 335 (12 April 1843).
4 Jenkins, *Church in Industrial Rhymney*, pp. 83f; E. T. Davies, *Religion and the Industrial Revolution in South Wales* (Cardiff, 1965), pp. 138f; Copleston Correspondence, to Traherne, no. 123 (10 October 1844). In fact 473 persons

were confirmed.

5   I. G. Jones, *Communities* (Llandysul, 1987), p. 180; Jones, *William Evans*, pp. 25-7.

6   *Church and People (Church Pastoral-Aid Society)*, VIII (1897) 220-2.

7   Jones, *William Evans*, p. 30; British Library, Gladstone Correspondence, Addit MS 44478 fol. 112, Lady Llanover to Gladstone, 16 December 1882.

8   *Report of the Royal Commission on the Church of England and other Religious Bodies in Wales and Monmouthshire*, volume II (London, 1910), p. 336.

9   Davies, *Religion in the Industrial Revolution*, pp. 138f; *Church and People*, pp. 220f; Jones, *William Evans*, p. 45; *Report of the Llandaff Diocesan Conference*, 1887, pp. 95-7. In the *CPAS Abstract of Report for 1887* (p. 23) Evans said, '(w)hen I open my mouth to speak it is needless to tell you that I am a Welshman just come up from Wales. I am a Welshman, a thorough Welshman, a Welshman of the Welsh.... I love its people, and I love its language; I speak to my fellow-countrymen every day, and I preach to them every week in their dear old mother tongue – the most melodious tongue on the face of the earth'. He also mentioned in this speech (p. 24) the implications of a bilingual policy, and was grateful that the CPAS both understood this and supported it.

10 Jones, *William Evans*, pp. 36-9; Evans's obituary in *Y Cyfaill Eglwysig*, 1900, pp. 238f; J. R. D. Williams, *The Parish of Rhymney, Centenary* (Cardiff, 1943), p. 1. Elwyn Bowen notes that Evans preached at the opening of Vaynor Church in the open-air to a congregation of about one thousand people (*Vaynor* (Merthyr Tydfil, 1992), p. 238).

11 Islwyn and Jean Jenkins, *Beyond the Black Tips* (Aberystwyth, 1990), pp. 248f; Jones, *William Evans*, pp. 40f.

12 Roger L. Brown, *Reviving the Clergy, Renewing the Laity: Archbishop Benson's Mission in Wales* (Welshpool, 1994), pp. 28f, 43, 48, 50, quoting, in part the Benson Papers (Lambeth Palace Library) 170, fols. 4f, 87f, 235; Jesse Jones speaking at the 1911 Llandaff Diocesan Conference, *Report*, pp. 83f, quotes Evans's remark to Benson, though in his *William Evans* he adds the words, 'Turn her directions straight to the Sun of Righteousness' (p. 36).

13 Ecclesiastical Commission papers, return of 1887 and other correspondence. In 1870 one of his curates, D. R. Jones, had his licence revoked on a charge of intoxication being proved against him.

14 For the details of the Llanover row see Jones, *William Evans*, pp. 47-53. The details regarding Gladstone's consideration of Evans for the episcopate are found in the Gladstone papers, Addit MS 44478, fols. 112 (Lady Llanover to Gladstone, 16 December 1882) and 195 (draft of Gladstone to Bishop Campbell, 28 December 1882).

15 *Church and People*, pp. 220-1; Davies, *Religion in the Industrial Revolution*, p. 139; *In Memoriam, Rev. David Edmondes Owen, Vicar of Llandovery 1911-22*, by J.T.D., p. 8.

16 Jones, *William Evans*, pp. 31-3, 54f; *Report of the Llandaff Diocesan Conference*, 1894, pp. 29f: it was also noted that Evans had written one of the best confirmation books in the Welsh language.

17 *Church Pastoral-Aid Society: Abstract of Report*, 1887, pp. 25-6.
18 Jones, *William Evans*, pp. 28f; Jenkins, *Beyond the Black Tips*, pp. 255f; Williams, *Parish of Rhymney*, p. 36; *Y Cyfaill Eglwysig*, 1900, pp. 238f.
19 Jenkins, *Beyond the Black Tips*, p. 248.
20 Quoted in Williams, *Parish of Rhymney*, p. 38.

The 'Welsh' Life of William Walsham How

The name of William Walsham How is known to most Christians in the English-speaking world as that of a hymnwriter. 'For all the Saints', or 'It is a thing most Wonderful', are probably his most familiar hymns. Yet How's reputation during his latter years, from the 1870s onwards, was more than that of a hymnwriter of some substance. He was also highly regarded as a mission speaker and evangelist, a writer of Christian literature, an enthuser of clergy, and as a leader in the forward movement of the Church, especially in the more difficult areas of East London and the industrial areas of Yorkshire. In addition, How may also be seen as a pioneer ecumenist. The seed of much of this work lay in How's quiet but significant ministry in a small country parish, that of Whittington, near Oswestry, with a population in the 1850s of 1,600 people. It is there, in its churchyard, that How was buried, although at the time of his death he was bishop of Wakefield and was a household name within the Church of England, a favourite of Queen Victoria, and one who had declined the premier see of Durham some years earlier. The parish of Whittington, although it is in Shropshire, was in his day, and until the disestablishment of the Church in Wales in 1920, part of the diocese of St Asaph. It is now part of the diocese of Lichfield. This is my reason for describing his ministry there as a 'Welsh' ministry, although I suspect that How would not have made such a claim, even though he was a canon of St Asaph Cathedral.

Born in 1823, at Shrewsbury, the son of a wealthy solicitor,

William Wybergh How, William Walsham How's family had Cumberland roots, his father's father, Peter How, being rector of Workington. As a day boy at Shrewsbury School, where he was a fellow-pupil of Bishop Basil Jones of St Davids and Bishop Fraser of Manchester, he was said to have been a favourite of his headmaster, the celebrated classical scholar, Dr Kennedy. It was in this school that his great love of botany was cultivated.

How went up to Oxford intending to follow his father in the legal profession, but his already strong Christian faith, and the influence of the Tractarian movement in the University (which attracted him although it never made him an adherent), made him change his mind and opt instead for ordination. A rather poor degree, a third, was awarded him, but being only twenty-one, when the minimum age for ordination was twenty-three, he took the unusual step of going to Durham University to read theology and to prepare for ordination there, especially as the course included some practical teaching.

Made deacon in 1846, How served his 'title' as curate of Kidderminster, under T. L. Claughton, who was later bishop of Rochester, and with whom he developed a long and lasting friendship. It may be that it was from Claughton that he gained his concern for practical religion and was encouraged to develop his gifts as a preacher. It was at Kidderminster that he found his wife, Frances Ann, who was the sister of one of his numerous fellow curates, and a daughter of Henry Douglas, rector of Salwarpe and canon of Durham. Before he married How moved back to Shrewsbury to serve as curate of Holy Cross, the Abbey parish, mainly because his stepmother had died and he wished to live at home and comfort his father. It was the custom of their home to read a sermon at the family's prayer time on Sunday. Instead, How composed his own sermons for these occasions, and these formed the basis of his first, and one of his most influential books, *Plain Words*, published in 1858.[1]

His son records in his life that on 23 September 1851, 'Walsham How was instituted by the Bishop of St. Asaph to the Rectory of Whittington in the county of Salop'. The words are selective, for by the time of his writing, 1899, the circumstances of his appointment to that parish were distinctly embarrassing, and had been the subject of substantial comment on different occasions. This was because How's father had purchased the next presentation to the living from its patron, Mrs Lloyd of Aston, in the parish of Selattyn. She was probably the widow of William Lloyd, and the daughter of Admiral Sir Elijah Harvey. Her husband's younger brother, Charles Arthur Albany Lloyd, was appointed rector of Whittington in 1809, and later held the other family living of Selattyn from 1846 until his death in 1851. Both parishes were wealthy, Selattyn being valued at £771, and Whittington at £1,000. As the incumbent was elderly (he was 65 in 1850) the prospect of an early vacancy was not unreasonable. This fact, together with the value of the living, ensured that the cost of purchasing the next presentation must have been considerable. The purchase allowed the purchaser to act as patron of the living for that presentation only, the advowson, or the right of appointment, continuing to be held by the Lloyd family. For Mrs Lloyd it was a ready way of obtaining a substantial sum of money; for Mr How, a way of forwarding the clerical career of his son and ensuring his temporal prosperity by a one-off payment. Although these arrangements were still legal at the time of purchase, probably between 1846 and 1851, they were coming under increasing censure from ecclesiastical reformers. Such men were disturbed that the care of immortal souls could be purchased for a financial payment, and that money, rather than merit, was the touchstone of appointment to the more lucrative livings.

It is not surprising, therefore, that on a number of occasions when How ventured to support the English establishment of the diocese of St Asaph, the Welsh-speaking clergy rudely reminded him about the circumstances of his own preferment.

In 1869, there was a public call for the bishop of St Asaph, Thomas Vowler Short, to take advantage of the recently passed Bishops' Resignation Act on the grounds of his anti-Welsh stance and his gross nepotism. In the bishop's defence, How wrote a letter to the *Guardian* which gave 'a warm eulogy upon the magnificence and unselfishness of the Bishop of St Asaph' in financially contributing to the work of his diocese the greater part of his episcopal income.

Cambro-Catholic, who replied to How's letter in the *Church Times*, having made clear that he was not a clergyman of that diocese, protested that however much this might be true, How was an Englishman and consequently could not understand the feelings of the Welsh people about Short's episcopate. He continued: '[t]he fact is, that Mr How is an Englishman who has purchased a living in an English portion of the Diocese of St Asaph. He is, therefore, no exponent of the sentiment and feeling of the Welsh people who form nine-tenths of the population of that diocese. I know of no single disinterested Welsh Churchman, and having the highest interests of the Church intelligently at heart, who could conscientiously sit down to write a panegyric on the Episcopate of the present Bishop of St Asaph.'

This was somewhat mild to the public rebuke How received in 1875. In that year David Howell of Cardiff was appointed vicar of Wrexham by Bishop Hughes of St Asaph. A group of St Asaph clergy vocally disagreed with Hughes's selection, arguing that it suggested that the bishop felt he had no clergy in his own diocese worthy of such a position. When How accused such men in turn of considering themselves worthy of promotion, he was accused by Venables Williams of Llandrillo, one of the more outspoken clerics in the diocese, of holding his own living, the wealthiest in the diocese, by purchase. It is significant that How never took a prominent part in the diocesan events and quarrels after these attacks on him.[2]

If this embarrassment prevented How playing any

substantial part in the predominately Welsh-speaking parts of the diocese, and confined him to its more English-speaking areas, his ministry at Whittington was nevertheless an outstanding success, if we are able to use such temporal terms about spiritual affairs. Although his son, in his biography, despises his predecessor as an adherent of the old evangelical school who had had texts of Scripture painted on the outside of the late Georgian red-brick church, and on cottage walls, it may well be that Lloyd's ministry was one upon which How was able to build. Lloyd's memorial tablet at Whittington reads that '[h]e most zealously preached Christ crucified, was a true and tried friend of the poor and most warmly and energetically advocated the cause of the Church Missionary Society, remembering and obeying the Scripture precept, "Tell it out among the brethren that the Lord is King" – Psalm xcvi., 10.' If this was true, then How succeeded a man who had proclaimed the same Gospel as he preached, cared for people, and reminded them about the Great Commission of our Lord.

What was true, however, was that the rectory house and grounds were in a deplorable state and needed much work on them to make them fit for the new incumbent. It was equally true that the hymn book in use at the church was a local effort, totally inadequate for a person of How's poetic sensibilities. The music was produced by a barrel organ, probably limited to a selection of tunes, the font was a shallow oval basis on a stand, and the chancel seating consisted of two long benches. How, who was described as a man of order and punctuality, soon corrected these so-called deficiencies, (though he followed Bishop Short's advice and determined to make no changes for a year until people knew him sufficiently to trust him), mapped out the parish, numbered every house, and indexed every person living in the parish together with their particulars. His curates, of whom he had one and often two, were provided with these details.[3]

Whittington was a parish which like any other of the period

– and Kilvert's Diary offers many examples – had its incidents of humour and even superstition. Some were recorded by How. Visiting an elderly couple soon after his becoming rector, the woman of the house told him:

> The old man and me, sir, never go to bed without singing the Evening Hymn. Not that I've got any voice left, for I haven't, and, as for him, he's like a bee in a bottle; and then he don't humour the tune, for he don't rightly know one tune from another, and he can't remember the words neither; so, when he leaves out a word, I puts it in, and when I can't sing I dances, and so we gets through it somehow.

There was also the occasion when, calling on a woman who was neighbour to a man who had just died, she remarked that she had seen him go past her house just after his death. Asking for particulars, she explained that had he walked down the road, in front of the house, and 'was exactly like a cat!' Suggesting to a farmer that perhaps they might use the family Bible, he was greeted with the answer, 'Thank goodness we never had an occasion for that sort of book for many a long year, ever since the old cow was so bad.'[4]

Throughout his 28 years residence at Whittington, How paid great importance to attending the parochial schools and to visiting his parishioners. The National Schools were built in 1854, replacing a former Lancasterian school held in a former tithe barn. His own practice was to attend the schools every morning at 9.00 a.m., and to make on average of around 30 or so home visits a week. As the parish was an extensive one, 7 miles from point to point, containing numerous hamlets and outlying farms and cottages, he rode a cob, often with one of his children on a pony by his side, on these visits. Nor did How make any distinction between church and chapel people, but visited all.

The worship of the Church was also improved, How training his own choir, using a flute for the accompaniment. At first the boys were dressed in Eton collars and bright blue ties. The old barrel organ, purchased in 1810, was finally superseded by a new organ in 1867. Extra celebrations of the Holy Communion and weekday evening services were also introduced. His services were described as conducted with a loyalty to the tenor of the Prayer Book, 'with no repellent badness on one hand, and no excessive ritual on the other'. One of his first 'reforms' was the presentation of a new font, given by himself, and a new pulpit and prayer desk, the latter given in memory of How's eldest son who had died at an early age in Barmouth. In 1860 open seats were substituted for several of the old pews in the nave, How himself paying the cost of this improvement, feeling no doubt that appropriated seats gave the wrong message about the Church caring for the poor as well as the rich. By 1871 he felt able to sweep all the old pews away, and again he bore most of the cost himself. In the following year he rebuilt the chancel at a cost of £165, which he paid himself, putting in choir stalls, though the north chancel aisle, then added, was paid for by public subscription. In addition How held cottage meetings in the more remote areas of his parish, where a service would be held and a sermon given. Not only were these services designed to reach out to people who found attendance at church difficult, they were also meant to hold people to the Church rather than allow them to join Nonconformity by default. His sermons were described as 'characterized by an admirable simplicity, both of matter and language, which fitted them for the congregation of a rural parish, and no one who heard them could fail to be impressed by the earnest tone of the preacher'. Some of his books indicate the truth of these remarks.

In order to get to know some of the older inhabitants of the parish an Old Men's Dinner was established from 1855 and held generally on New Year's Day. It was a time of cheerfulness, and various customs grew up with the event, such as toasting a man who had been born with the century, and singing a song called 'To-morrow'. But it was also a time when How was able to speak some solemn words to his guests. Equally, there was an annual tea for the older women, the usual school feasts, and the numerous concerts and lectures which every parish held. Many of these lectures were given by How, and they included such subjects as geology, his visit to Rome, modern poets, Sir Humphrey Davy, or astronomy.

Guilds too were established. How even gave his cook membership of the Guild of Church Workers, an honour in which she delighted. How explained it was given because she made delicacies for the poor in her own time, with the result that her work was as valuable as that of any district visitor who took them in person to the recipient.

There was also an occasion for church extension in his parish, and in 1858 St Andrew's Church, Frankton, was consecrated. A new parish of Welsh Frankton was later formed with St Andrew's becoming the parish church. A district chapel was built at Ebnal in 1869. How's letter of invitation to 'The Christian Inhabitants of Frankton', dated August 1858, was an invitation for them to attend this new church, seating 200 in free seats, with two services and two sermons each Sunday. "[A]ll are welcome," he wrote, who will come to hear the sound of the Gospel of Christ, to receive His Sacraments, and to worship Him, according to the precept of St. Paul, "decently and in order". Does this not seem to be an invitation to us all to draw nearer together in the worship of our God and Saviour, and to put an end to some of those *differences in religion* which keep us apart from one another?'

It was a call for Christians to unite together, for all professed to worship the same God and Saviour, all fought against the same enemies, and all hoped to meet in the same place and see God face to face. Far better to stand together in order to attack the enemies of Christianity. Church people, he continued, bore no malice against those who differed from them, and he believed that the same applied to most Nonconformists. Rather, How wrote:

> We only long to see them [Nonconformists] worshipping God by our sides once more, as our forefathers worshipped; and we believe that very few among them really differ from us so much as to be unable to worship God in a Church. We do not wish to tie people down against their will to a particular form of worship which they do not like, or refuse to any Christian 'liberty of conscience'; but we cannot read our Bibles without learning again and again that it is Christ's will that His Church should be *one*, and we cannot think of this without feeling sad and ashamed that there are so *many* sects and parties among us. Surely, when we think of Our Saviour, we must all long and pray for unity. *We* pray for it continually, and we believe others do so too. Can we expect God to hear our prayers, if we do not *strive* for it as well? And is not this an opportunity which seemed to call upon us to do something towards drawing nearer together?

There was no worship 'more beautiful, more spiritual, more scriptural, than that of the Church of England', and How asked all those who read his leaflet to be 'no longer at variance in worshipping Him' but to follow the precept of Christ and 'be ONE'. It is not known what response he achieved with this moderate and compassionate appeal, so different from the strictures placed upon Nonconformity by many other parochial clergymen.

Speaking on the subject of lay agency for the work of the Church in relationship to country parishes, at the Stoke on Trent Church Congress of 1875, How maintained that in a country parish, tact, gentleness, and consideration for others, were of special importance, and it was far better to give way in matters 'not of principle' than to risk losing confidence, support and perhaps one's fellow workers. This was because 'the smaller the population the greater was the importance of each individual', while rural people were generally more 'straitened in their views and of less expanded sympathies' than town dwellers. Furthermore they could not readily find another church as could those living in towns.

His paper, undoubtedly based on his experience and work at Whittington, gave a number of hints about gaining the support of the laity in such rural parishes as his own. While he doubted the expediency of parochial councils he considered it important that clergy should consult with their leading lay people. He equally commended pastoral visiting, suggesting to the younger clergy in similar parishes to his own that not only should they visit systematically, but they should also seize upon every pretext for making a visit, especially when they knew they had been some misunderstanding or annoyance with their ministry.

How suggested that a Guild of Church Workers should be formed, comprising such people as Sunday school teachers, choir members, district visitors, collectors, 'and any others whom I could find an excuse for enrolling as Church-workers' (such as his cook). Let the clergyman take these people into his confidence, show deference to their reasonable requests, arrange quarterly meetings and an anniversary day, with a celebration of the Holy Communion in the morning and a social gathering in the evening, followed by a service in church and a special address. Although there might not be many in a rural community, if any, who could conduct cottage lectures or act as a lay reader, many could be encouraged to give out tracts (which he once despised, but now knew better), or to collect subscriptions to missionary societies or similar organisations.

A Society of Holy Living too might be formed, with a view to mutual help in holiness of living. Even if such a group – possibly only three or four people – met monthly on a Sunday, to read some devotional book and pray, the influence and example of 'a nucleus of devout people with a high and holy aim' would tell upon others. Equally, How urged the use of the Church's daily prayer as a service open and available to all. Few might be able to attend, but he knew from practical experience how two or three hard working mothers of families appreciated 'the peaceful twenty minutes thus given from time to time to God'.

The need to imitate the dissenters in establishing mission centres in scattered areas was also commended. Let mission rooms and school-churches be multiplied as far as possible, How suggested, and even though there might be difficulties in arranging Sunday services they should do the best they could. The use of distant farm houses for a similar purpose was also suggested, especially when accompanied by personal invitations given out a few days beforehand. Nevertheless, the parish church should always remain the centre of the spiritual life of the parish, but services needed to 'be very hearty, very simple, very reverent, very congregational; and let our preaching be very plan, very earnest, and very practical'. High standards were still required even when there was little response, for 'If there are few that will listen, the servant is not faring worse than the Master; and the saving of one soul is worth a life's labour'.

The country parish also permitted the opportunity of being closely involved in the local school, opening it with prayer and conducting the religious teaching. It allowed the cleric the opportunity of adapting himself to the modes of thoughts and expressions familiar to the poor, and was of utmost value to the pupils concerned. Children's services should not be neglected. Short, bright musical services, with children's hymns to popular tunes, and a short sermon illustrated by stories and enlivened by catechising, and delivered from the chancel steps rather than the pulpit, were some of How's suggestions. Arguing that the Sunday school should be held on a Sunday morning, he suggested that the children should be brought into

William Evans of Rhymney

David Jones of Penmaenmawr

Willian Latham Bevan

readers, librettos and lec
science. One favourite pu;
the late Sir DANIEL MO
sometime Head of Kew Gar
knighted for investigation:
the condition of coffee pla
the West Indies. Town no
than School will honour F
Cole's public service as new
the School Board, general secretary and ins;
of the Board Schools, librarian of the Free L

THE SCHOOLMASTER HAS I
sponsor in the equally ample personalit;
Revd. EDWARD BURNARD SQUIRE
Vicar of St Mary's, whose life-work it is to I
the schooling of eleven hundred children.]
move Oxford Street sets education in a mo
adequate setting, on a worthier scale than h
at York Place. A voluntary subscription of £
commanding the appropriate grant from My
at Whitehall, is a tribute to the exertions
Vicar and the example of the Church. That e
stays on for the 61,987 children who pass th
its schools by 1904: 34,959 at Oxford Street
13,192 at Parochial (1862), 5,705 at Christ Churc

*Edward Squire, drawn from a contemporary illustration by the late
W. Emlyn Davies, and reproduced from the anniversary booklet for the
National Schools, Swansea, 1848-1948*

William Walsham How as Bishop of Wakefield

Llansamlet parish church before its rebuilding (credit unknown).

Ellis Owen Ellis's cartoon of R.W. Morgan (holdubg a leek) drives Bishops Short, Thirlwall and Ollivant over Offa's Dyke and into a fiery dragon's mouth (credit: National Library of Wales and Peter Lord)

church for part of the service, and he advised that a child should never be passed without 'a pleasant smile of recognition'.

Such was his advice, and from what we have already learnt about his ministry at Whittington, this was advice that had been faithfully put into practice during his own experience of rural ministry.

It was a joint ministry as well, for his wife assisted him. She carried on the usual mothers' meetings and clothing clubs, and was a pioneer of the Girls' Friendly Society, but she also nursed the sick, and if one was ill, night or day, wet or fine, people did not hesitate to summon her. It is said that her watchful care preserved many a life, and the asthma and bronchitis which caused her death, eight years after they left the parish, was attributed to her over exertion during a mission in the parish.

How also played a significant part in his nearest town, Oswestry, being a valued member of the Literary Institute, often lecturing for them, while he also gave much support to the Church of England Young Men's Society which had a branch in the town. The Oswestry and Welshpool Naturalists Field Club, we are told, also looked upon How as a leader, 'in whose absence the excursions are never anything like so pleasant or so profitable'. His intellectual stimulus, reported a local newspaper, was sorely needed in the town, and his departure from it would be a great loss.

In 1879 Walsham How was appointed bishop of Bedford, and preached his farewell sermon at Whittington on 7 September. While he thanked God for the fellowship in the Gospel he had received in the parish, he would not pretend that all had been bright and hopeful, for he knew that in his own life there had much that had been left undone and other things had been done 'slackly and unworthily'. But he would look on the joys and encouragements too, especially of 'the dear, dear friends who so often had spoken to him of their souls, and whom he had seen growing and persevering, and coming nearer and nearer to their God'. This care was reciprocated for at another presentation to him, Edmund Wright of Halston said that he did not believe there had been any 'interruption of that friendly intercourse which has existed between the pastor and his flock for twenty-eight years'.[5]

This period of 28 years service in a rural parish is not an isolated one, and was matched by many clergymen who brought in new styles of worship, new standards of service, an enhanced sense of pastoral care and duty, and an earnest desire to do the best for the spiritual and moral welfare of their parishioners. What perhaps made it different from most was How's sense of moderation and his concern for each individual. This was seen especially in his desire for unity with the Nonconformists of Frankton, and also his ability to encourage others, by example, and by the written and spoken word, to follow in the same steps. As such he was a mentor to numerous clergy, especially the younger and probably English-speaking clergy of the diocese of St Asaph. But there were other reasons why How was offered a bishopric in 1879 (as well as on previous occasions), over and above this parochial work and his influence over his fellow clergymen. These reasons may be described as his work as a retreat organiser and mission conductor, a writer of Christian works, and as a moderate force in the counsels of the Church.

How was concerned not only about deepening the spiritual life of his parishioners, but also that of the clergy. The clergy, gaining spiritual insight and confidence, could then impart when they had found for themselves to their own parishioners. It was a key work. It appears that Archdeacon Ffoulkes of Llandyssil, in Montgomeryshire (who succeeded How at Whittington) was one of the pioneers of these clergy retreats. By the summer of 1869 two or three of these retreats had been held at his rectory, and How suggested that one could be held at Whittington, with the clergy staying at the Rectory or in nearby accommodation. Edward King, then principal of Cuddesdon

College, a theological college in the high church tradition near Oxford, and later bishop of Lincoln, was the guest conductor. On this occasion a considerable newspaper controversy resulted as rumours circulated that the clergy were meeting for the purpose of celebrating the Roman mass.

How was sufficiently impressed by this retreat to continue this work, and also to extend it to those men who were about to be ordained at Lichfield Cathedral. As an examining chaplain to the bishop of Lichfield, How was responsible for examining the candidates prior to ordination, which meant that some might fail within a day or two of the eventual ordination. His own concern was to ensure that there was a more spiritual approach to this event, and thus he established a pre-ordination retreat. He also made similar arrangements for the ordinations at Rochester Cathedral, whose bishop was his former vicar.

By the 1860s missions had become a feature of church life in England, Bishop Wilberforce of Oxford being regarded as one of the pioneers of this work. He had organised parochial missions in the more populous centres of his diocese from the 1850s onwards. A great mission to London in 1869, although conducted by Anglo-Catholics, received such favourable comment that another was held in 1874, while Moody and Sankey were first invited to England with their American-style evangelistic mission in 1873. Important missions were held in Cardiff and Swansea in 1870, which had notable results, bringing in new converts and giving a new impetus to the life of the local churches.

Preparing his own parish for a mission in 1873, How wrote that missions were 'a sort of Church "revival", conducted generally (not always) upon sober Church principles. In some particulars, especially in the prayer-meetings, they startle, and even offend, old-fashioned Church people of conservative instincts, but they win souls for Christ, and deepen the reality and earnestness of many.' His own experience of the missions he had conducted had convinced him that they could bring the greatest possible blessing to a parish. At this mission, which justified its expectations, it was said of How that his concern for personal religion came out markedly in the after meetings held after the main meeting. Speaking with the utmost reverence and earnestness of voice and manner, he begged people to pray for themselves, and while they remained on their knees he would walk quietly up and down the church, uttering Scriptural verses of help and encouragement.

The first mission he conducted was at North Malvern in 1872, and although he expressed diffidence about undertaking it, he added 'if he could be of any use to a brother, specially to one young in the ministry, he would, God helping him, do his best'. Assisted by Canon Howell Evans, vicar of Oswestry, he worked with quiet earnestness. His mission sermons were pointed but persuasive. The after meetings were quiet and reverent, free from excitement but most impressive. His morning instructions on the spiritual life helped many to live closer to God and persevere more hopefully. Thereafter he conducted a number of missions each year until he became a bishop, where his simple affectionate earnestness rather than his brilliant oratory, 'the largeness of his sympathy, and the sunniness of his smile', won people's hearts. Humility and holiness shone out of him and his tenderness in dealing with souls, it was said, made many people seek him out as a man whom God had sent to them in order to lead them to Himself.[6]

His books too had made How's name well known throughout the Church. His first work, *Plain Words, or Sixty Short Sermons for the Poor and for Family Reading*, first published in 1858, and its three sequels, went through innumerable editions. The first volume was divided into four parts. The first related to specific seasons, the second to the groundwork of religion, such as sin and conversion, atonement and justification. The third related to sins and duties, and the last to the Christian's 'daily walk'. It was written in the same way as he spoke, it appears, with a directness and yet with a warmth of sympathy and understanding. The great question is not whether we were converted once but whether we are new creatures now, he wrote, stating that there should be no mistake here for it was a matter of life and death. 'Are we living the *new life*? Do we know what it is by the experience of our own hearts? Do we really love God? Do we honestly hate sin? Do we feel to God as children should feel to a loving Father? Have we any faith in Christ? Does the Atonement made by Him for us make any difference in us?' were some of the questions he asked. If such questions could be answered aright 'we need not fear; God is with us, and no power in heaven or earth, or in hell itself, "shall be able to separate us from the love of God which is in Christ Jesus our Lord".'

From 1863-8 How worked on a commission from the Church publishers, The Society for Promoting Christian Knowledge, for a commentary on the four gospels. This commentary was immensely popular and nearly a quarter of a million copies were sold. In 1874 what was probably How's most influential book was published, *Pastor in Parochiâ*. This was a manual for clergy of prayers and readings, for use on such occasions as the visiting and the communion of the sick, private baptisms, confessions and absolutions. It included such services as a litany for one who was unconscious, a service for the dying, prayers after a death, and prayers and readings for children, together with a selection of hymns. It is said that probably nine out of ten of the younger clergy were brought up on it, and it is known that Archbishop Longley of Canterbury, on his death bed, was much comforted by some of the readings and prayers from it. Four years later appeared another influential book or booklet. This was his manual for the Holy Communion. It was reprinted over and over again until the 1930s. These books were written in the midst of parish life, and one of How's curates wrote that he make time for literary work by employing odd moments at his writing desk, having the greatest horror of wasting any time. Other works included *The Parish Priest, Daily*

Family Prayers for Churchmen, Freedom for Colonial Churches, The Ballad of the Chorister Boy and *The Boy Hero.*

A poet by inclination, How was able to write serious and humorous verse, much of which appeared in the *Spectator* under his initials. Some were republished in a book entitled *Three All Saints' Summers.* How excelled, however, in the writing of hymns, and while many of them have passed into oblivion because of their Victorian sentimentality and mawkishness, some have survived. With Thomas Baker Morrell he edited and published in 1854 *Psalms and Hymns.* To this How contributed several items, including a passion hymn occasionally sung today, 'Lord Jesu, when we stand afar'. His passiontide hymn for children, 'It is a thing most wonderful', appeared in a church hymnbook for children in 1873, while his mission hymn, 'O Jesus, Thou art standing', was published in a supplement to the 1854 book in 1867. His best known hymn, 'For all the Saints who from their Labours rest', was published in 1864. These hymns, according to Julian's *Dictionary of Hymnody*, were 'simple, unadorned, but enthusiastically practical hymns', and all of them were written in his Whittington days. How was also joint-editor of the SPCK *Church Hymns*, which was long the most formidable rival of *Hymns Ancient and Modern*, and used by those who found the latter too sacramental and high church in tone.

Although these activities made him well-known to many, it is said that How came into prominence in 1867 when he was asked at short notice by Canon Erskine Clarke, one of the most influential of Victorian clerics, to speak in a debate on church ceremonial at the Wolverhampton Church Congress of that year. These congresses were unofficial but highly influential meetings, designed to bring all church parties together and to introduce new thinking to the Church at large.

The problem How was asked to address was a local one, but had national implications, namely how to keep different sets of people, high churchmen and evangelicals, together in the same

Church. His subsequent address was described as 'epoch making'. He endorsed the Tractarian concern for its love of more beautiful and attractive services, its concern for daily prayer and the centrality of the Eucharist, and in passing noted the doctrine which lay behind it. Yet he protested about the 'scornful superiority' with which this party held its views, especially by claiming that those who did not belong to it were 'mere Anglicans' who held only a small portion of Catholic truth. Furthermore How refused to narrow the name 'Catholic' to 'a party watchword':

> We love the doctrine of the Church as we love nothing else, believing it to be 'the truth as it is in Jesus'; we refuse to narrow it to mean Church doctrine as set forth in one particular development, and in one peculiar phraseology. We desire to treat candidly, and in a spirit of brotherly love, those with whom we find ourselves unable to agree in many things. And we desire to remain, what we hope we are now, plain, faithful, honest members of our ancient and purified, and therefore dearly beloved, Church of England.

In the words of his son, '[t]his speech established his position in the Church as one who could not brook slovenliness or inadequacy in her services any more than he could approve the practices of the extreme Ritualistic party'. The *Guardian*, a church paper, commented that if it had not been for How's speech 'it would have seemed as if the old English *via media*, with its long array of orators and divines, its massive learning and dignified intensity of character, had no place in a Church Congress of our time'. How, in fact, always maintained that he was a moderate high churchman.[7]

His integrity as a clergyman, his moderation and winning manners, his record of publications, as well as his gifts of leadership and his ability to win friends, ensured that How was brought into prominence in the diocese in which he served. In

1852 he became a diocesan inspector of schools for St Asaph, and in 1854 rural dean of Oswestry (on his first visitation he found three of its churches without fonts). In 1860 he was appointed a prebendary of the cathedral, and in 1877 he became chancellor, that is, one of its dignitaries. In 1868-9, possibly as a result of his Church Congress address, he was nominated as Select Preacher at Oxford, and in 1869 his fellow clergy elected him as a proctor for his diocese to Convocation, the Church's parliament. Nine years later he was appointed examining chaplain to the bishop of Lichfield.

As proctor he was placed on numerous committees of Convocation. Amongst them were the committees for the new translation of the Bible (which appeared as the Revised Version); the revision of the Athanasian Creed; and one on rubrics, a controversial subject, in which he advocated that the Tractarians should give up those robes which held doctrinal significance, but that the evangelicals should accept more ceremonial in worship provided it had the sanction of the bishops. By this time he was being offered a number of overseas bishoprics, amongst them Natal and Capetown, which he declined, as well as a number of preferments within the Church of England.

In 1878 How was sounded out for a new suffragan bishopric designed to serve the East London area. As it was thought at the time that only bishoprics which had been created in medieval times could be re-established, the title of his suffragan see was that of the bishopric of Bedford. After a hiccup caused by Queen Victoria being told that he taught private confession, which was untrue, How was appointed to the suffragan see, where he made a considerable impact, and became known as the omnibus bishop, for his use of that method of transport. In 1888 he became the first bishop of Wakefield, and did much to put the new diocese on its feet, even inviting the Community of the Resurrection to make its home at Mirfield. But his episcopal life is another story.[8]

His wife's health meant that even in the Whittington years they had to spend considerable parts of the winter abroad, while his family made Barmouth their centre for an annual summer holiday. A keen fisherman, How fished both the Ceriog and the Tanat rivers. His will indicated that he left a sum of £72,240, but as sensitive as ever, How added a note to it stating that he had inherited substantially from his father and his wife's parents, had used most of his episcopal income for his diocesan work, had always given away the royalties on his books, and had tithed what remained. It was said on the debit side that he found it difficult to say 'no', especially to a personal applicant, and he would decide important matters with what appeared to be reckless haste. It was claimed that young men found him cold and reserved, and with the squirearchy he would not speak his mind as he ought. On the other hand, How stated, modestly, that he was too busy to do his work thoroughly, and he was not 'an exemplary or successful parish priest'.

In many respects How was a typical Victorian, with a strong streak of sentimentality which appears in his hymns and addresses. Equally, he believed that the Church's duty was not only to help people lead better and more hopeful lives, but also to teach the working classes patience and unselfishness. Yet he could also argue in the same speech that the Church needed to be more concerned about the daily life of its people. In a speech to the Church Congress at Rhyl in 1891, How argued that the Church's teaching needed to be plain, manly and definite, and it needed to discuss not abstract questions but the real issues of the day, often matters of right and justice, life and morals. It was no use preaching a religion that floated over the heads of ordinary people and never touched their daily lives. Let people see that the Church was a divine society, welcoming, congregational in its worship, with earnest and real preaching, and such people would find that she was 'God's instrument for blessing and purifying and ennobling their life here, as well as for preparing them for an infinitely better life hereafter'.[9]

It is for such practical statements that How will be remembered, and equally for placing a warm and human face upon the Church itself. And much of the preparation for that work came from his extensive and lengthy ministry in a rural Shropshire parish.

ENDNOTES

1   Frederick Douglas How, *Bishop Walsham How* (London, 1899), pp. 11-42.
2   Ibid, p 43; Mrs Bulkeley Owen, *History of the Parish of Selattyn* (Oswestry, nd), pp. 28, 407f; *Church Times*, 12 November 1869, p. 439; *Wrexham Guardian*, 27 February 1875, p. 7, 6 March 1875, p. 4, 13 March 1875, p. 7.
3   How, *Bishop Walsham How*, pp. 44-5, 52f; Owen, *Selattyn*, p. 408.
4   How, *Bishop Walsham How*, pp. 46f; F D How (ed), *Lighter Moments from the Notebook of Bishop Walsham How* (London, 1900), pp. 13, 16, 24 especially.
5   How, *Bishop Walsham How*, pp. 49-52, 88, 148-51; *By-Gones*, 18 August 1897, pp. 178f; newspaper cuttings in National Library of Wales, D. R. Thomas papers, on How's appointment to the bishopric of Bedford, and on the death of his wife, SA/DR/50, fol. 213, and SA/DR/51, fol. 75; *Report of the Stoke on Trent Church Congress*, 1875, pp. 324-8; *To the Inhabitants of Frankton*, in SA/DR/51, fol. 29.
6   How, *Bishop Walsham How*, pp. 95-108; Roger L. Brown, *Reviving the Clergy: Renewing the Laity* (Welshpool, 1994), pp. 12-15. In his later years How was known to take children's missions on the beach at Barmouth: How, *Bishop Walsham How*, p. 430.
7   How, *Bishop Walsham How*, pp. 52, 58-63, 381-417; W. W. How, *Plain Words* (38th edn, London, nd), pp. 166-8; W. W. How, *Pastor in Parochiâ* (7th edn, London, 1927).
8   How, *Bishop Walsham How*, pp. 50, 63f, 71-86, 109f, 134; *Bye-Gones*, 18 August 1897, pp. 178f.
9   How, *Bishop Walsham How*, pp. 88f; *Bye-Gones*, 17 November 1897, p. 233; *Report of the St Asaph Diocesan Conference*, 1890, p. 26; *Report of the Church Congress at Rhyl*, 1891, pp. 113-17.

A Forgotten Patriot
The Reverend David Jones [1848-1909]
of Penmaenmawr

Writing in 1980, Emlyn Sherrington considered that David Jones's major polemical work, *The Welsh Church and Welsh Nationality* of 1893, and other similar works, helped 'form the basis of a reactionary Welsh nationalism which blossomed around the turn of the century and which, through its three greatest exponents, J. Arthur Price, an Anglican barrister and two parish priests, the reverends A. W. Wade-Evans and J. E. de Hirsch-Davies, was to exert a powerful and profound influence on the early Welsh Nationalist Party'.[1] While I am not entirely convinced about Sherrington's thesis that these writers were influenced by thinkers of the French right, though some clearly were, he does point to the significance of David Jones as a formulator of a theory about Welsh history which had particular significance in Wales during the earlier decades of this century. But who was David Jones?

His portrait, reproduced in an obituary in *Y Cyfaill Eglwysig*,[2] written by his successor in its editorial chair, Maurice Roberts, indicates an elderly man, with white hair and beard. It comes as a shock to learn that Jones was 61 when he died. Roberts considered him a good example of a man who had striven manfully against many difficulties.

Born in the Llangeitho district, the heartland not only of Welsh Methodism but also of evangelical Church life, the example of his mother's godliness, and her teaching and prayers, had a profound effect on his character. He was baptised at Gwynfel Chapel, Llangeitho, so presumably he came from Nonconformist stock. His father was described as a labourer. Without any advantages of education, save presumably that of a local school, he joined 'the sons of labour' of that area, working as a farm labourer. Like many other sons of that area a vocation to the ministry of the Church was nurtured in him, so that at the age of 19 or 20, according to Morris, he started to prepare for entry to St David's College, Lampeter. How Jones did so is not clear: his name is not recorded amongst the 'best known alumni' of Ystrad Meurig school, although it is accepted the list is not complete.[3] This school specialised in preparing older men for entry to that college and would have been an obvious place for him to attend. One assumes he himself read up the subjects required for the entry examination, probably assisted by some friendly local clergy. It was certainly an ambitious undertaking, and the habit of hard study never left him.

At Lampeter Jones was a Welsh Church exhibitioner, becoming the senior scholar in his final year. This probably eased, if it did not erase, the financial costs and sacrifices of his three year degree course. He thus graduated in 1875 at the age of 27, which enabled him to be ordained immediately after graduation, though yet another examination was required of him, namely that imposed by the bishop's chaplains. It is significant that he took a degree, for most men in his position took a two-year course, which gave them a licentiate in divinity.

Ordained into the diocese of Bangor, not his home diocese, David Jones served as assistant curate in three parishes for a total period of seven years – an unusually short time, which suggests he had been marked out already as a man of some distinction. His first curacy was at Pistyll, linked with Edern, near Pwllheli, whose rector was Eleazar Williams, one of the leading evangelical clergy in the diocese of Bangor. When his rector moved to be vicar of Llangefni in Anglesey in 1877 David Jones went with him as curate, moving however in 1879 to be curate in the parish of Llandyffnan, a neighbouring parish, with a population of 1,300 odd. In 1882 the Lord Chancellor (who generally sought nominations from the diocesan bishops) presented Jones to the Anglesey parish of Newborough, with a population of just under a thousand, and an income of £250. Six years later the bishop of Bangor presented Jones to the more important living of Llanfair-Pwll-Gwyngyll with Llandysilio (Menai-Bridge), with its combined population of about two and a half thousand, where two curates assisted him. The income, surprisingly, was said to be £233, though this was probably the net income, after some deduction had been made for the rector's share of the curates' stipends. Roberts remarks that his restoration of the church at Newborough made it one of the ornaments of Anglesey. A further mark of his bishop's confidence in him came when he briefly served as rural dean of the Menai deanery, though this had to be vacated when he left Newborough. In addition Jones served as a lecturer at St Mary's Teachers' Training College, Bangor, between 1894-7.

In 1895 David Jones was presented by the private patron, Arthur Evill, to the quarrying parish and seaside 'watering place' of Dwygyfylchi – better known as Penmaenmawr. It had roughly the same population as his previous parish, and a slightly better income, but its relationship to the Gladstone family, who had kept a holiday home there for many years, made it a rather prestigious appointment. He was to remain here until his death in 1909.

His ministry was clearly an evangelical one. At Llanfair it is said that his ministry brought 'resurrection' to many, while at Penmaenmawr Roberts declared that he watched over the spiritual welfare of his people like a father to his children. We know a fair amount about Jones's work at Penmaenmawr as he was called as a witness to the Welsh Church Commission. Jones gave his evidence in 1907 though it was not published until 1911. This commission had been established through the influence of David Lloyd George as a compromise or stalling operation against the radical dissenters who wished to disestablish the four dioceses in Wales (collectively known as the Church in Wales) from the Province of Canterbury. Jones's inquisition by the commissioners displays all the reasons why the commission failed to find any solution to the religious problems of the nation, though its report is an outstanding account of the state of religion in Wales at the turn of the century. There was a dogmatic chairman, who failed to keep control or even sometimes to understand the statements made by witnesses; a hostile Nonconformist commissioner, J. Morgan Gibbon, who sought to extend the rules on every possible occasion, and Lord Hugh Cecil and Archdeacon Owen Evans who sought to interpret the evidence in as friendly a light to the Established Church as was possible.

Jones reported that his parish consisted of a large quarrying population, with a number of lodging-house keepers 'on the seaboard' and a few of the professional class, but 'with a considerable increase of summer visitors'. It was still predominately a Welsh-speaking area. He had two curates, both Welsh-speaking and funded by grants from the Church Pastoral-Aid Society and offertories. St Seiriol's Church, one of its three churches, was the English church of the parish. It had a large influx of summer worshippers, so that the church was often full during those months, though there was still a sufficiently large English population to ensure its survival if the visitors left. Many of the regular attenders were English people who had retired to the parish on account of their health. St Gwynan's was the Welsh Church, while St David's Church had services in the Welsh language and stood 'in the midst of the working men's houses'.

Eight ladies from the congregation acted as district visitors, and there were mothers' meetings, children's meetings (at which temperance was a feature), two Bible classes and a church instruction class, attended by grown-ups and young men. The Parochial Church Council, then a rather novel institution, had been established some years earlier, and appeared to be open to all church people and at which the work of the parish was discussed and promoted. Jones felt, in answer to questions, that the laymen of the Church could do much to assist the clergy in their religious work, and instanced that many of his men visited people and prayed with the sick in their homes. Further questioning revealed that Jones started his prayer meetings with the Lord's Prayer, then a hymn, followed by short responses; a chapter of Scripture was read and expounded for fifteen minutes, and then various laymen present were asked to give out a hymn or to pray, sometimes extempore, sometimes not. Between 12 and 50 attended, and in addition there was a regular Thursday night service. There had been some co-operation with the local Nonconformist churches with regard to the Bible Society, the Religious Tract Society and the local nursing institution.

During the previous ten years substantial sums had been raised and these were itemised: restoring and enlarging the parish church of St Seiriol, £2,000; enlarging and repairing the National Schools, £630; erecting the new Welsh church of St David's, £3,050 (Mrs Gladstone had opened a bazaar in aid of its funds); paying off the debt on the Vicarage field, £834; and donations given for home and foreign mission work, £1,100. It is said that Jones was extremely effective in raising money for these causes, as well as for promoting church schools and the church press. At the time of his death it was said that he had raised over £20,000 in his parish for church causes, and had put in order the National schools which, with its 500 children, was the largest school in the diocese.

Jones also alleged that in his parish, where there were bilingual forms of worship, and where Welsh-speaking children were introduced to the English Prayer Book in elementary schools, a large number of Welsh-speakers were attending English-language services. Furthermore, those who had gone to live in London or Liverpool found no difficulty in linking with an English-speaking church.

It was remarked of David Jones in his obituary that he had fulfilled many charitable duties in his parish, and was a true friend to his parishioners. His love of and ability in music saw an outlet in his presidency of the Penmaenmawr Male Voice Choir. He encouraged his parishioners to take part in the 1905 Revival, which had a powerful impact upon the life of his Welsh congregations (though as we note later, he expressed some concerns about its impact). He was a true parish priest, who gained the respect and affection of church people and Nonconformists, wrote Roberts, but also a man, we may reply, who had good sense to put some of his energies and abilities elsewhere, for the benefit of the wider Church.[4] This particular work related to his gifts as a preacher and, even more prominently, to his work as an author and editor.

Canon Jones, for he became a prebendary of Bangor Cathedral towards the end of his life and also rural dean of Arllechwedd, was known throughout North Wales as an outstanding preacher in both languages. Roberts recalled that sermons he had heard him preach in 1876-7, as a young man, were still remembered by him and by many others. His texts were evangelical ones, 'You must be born again', 'Come unto me all ye that labour'. His concern for preaching and its dignity and importance stemmed from his childhood, for he remembered being told that above Daniel Rowland's pulpit at Llangeitho was the text, 'How dreadful is this place'. Roberts, in pointing out that while he accepted many invitations to preach, claimed that Jones never neglected his own parish. It is an argument which suggests that some thought he did. There is also one reference that Jones acted as a missioner for parish missions. This was in 1893 when he was one of two missioners who conducted a very successful eight day mission at Llangadwaladr. His colleague was James Davies, rector of the Welsh Church in Liverpool. There were probably other occasions as well.[5]

****

David Jones's major work, for which he will be remembered, lay in the writing of books and the editing of a monthly journal. We will look at his books later on, but even their titles are significant. His first published work was an edition of the papers of Henry T. Edwards, a former and controversial dean of Bangor. This book appeared in 1887 with a biographical sketch of Dean Edwards, under the title *Wales and the Welsh Church*. For some reason Jones's name was not mentioned on the title page, but only in the 'advertisement', but he included the work on the title pages of his other publications. In one sense it is a surprising work, for Edwards was a high churchman and Jones an evangelical, but both were deeply concerned about the need for the Welsh Church to be thoroughly Welsh rather than being simply an extension of the Church of England in Wales. They longed for the indigenous nature of their Church, and both were men who believed in preaching, prayer and temperance.

If Jones was not immune to the dean's defects – his impulsiveness, his want of restraint, his impatience and his controversial statements and mannerisms – he warmed to him for his concern for clerical training (which Jones no doubt knew he lacked), and perhaps tried to make him out to be what he was not, an evangelical-Tractarian mishmash. As such he wrote about his hero's 'commanding presence, his undisguised and undaunted patriotism, his intense but unaffected love for Wales and Welsh people, his unfeigned partiality for our national institutions, his knowledge of the language, history, and temperament of the race from which he sprang, and, above all, his firm attachment to the Cymric Church'. And in recalling his death (though he does not mention that he died by his own hand) Jones wrote: 'The nation has lost in him a sincere patriot;

the Welsh Church a devoted son, and her most valiant defender; the pulpit a bright ornament, and his friends one whom they loved and admired.' Here is hero worship, and evidence that Edwards was able to attract around him men of different theological persuasions in the interests of an indigenous Welsh Church. Perhaps, too, there is a feeling of dismay, for Jones definitely wrote, as others also believed, that had Dean Edwards lived he would have become a bishop. And even if Jones had no personal ambition for himself, which is rather unlikely for he was a human being after all, he clearly believed that 'Bishop' Edwards would have led the Welsh Church into a glorious future. The mitre went instead to Edwards's younger brother, and he led the Church into another direction with fatal consequences.

Significantly, it was noted that before his death Jones was gathering information for another biography, that of David Howell, dean of St Davids, yet another irenic figure in the Welsh Church with a vision and purpose much like that of Dean Edwards. If Howell stood on the evangelical side of that movement, he was yet able to embrace other men of good will, as did Dean Edwards from his side of the theological fence.[6]

In 1893 Jones published *The Welsh Church and Welsh Nationality*. The more detailed study required for its writing, he claimed, had strengthened the conviction he had expressed in his life of Edwards. This was that the Welsh Church would never be able to assert her privileges, discharge her duties, never live down long-seated prejudices or refute the calumnies disseminated against her, never vindicate her claims, never win over the Welsh people, 'or effectively convince the nation of the divine authority of her commission, till her superior clergy, and those who hold her prominent offices, are able to address the masses with fluent efficiency in the vernacular'. He believed it was his duty to the Church to establish the validity of this argument and to publish his book. It was a brave decision. A writer in the *Caernarvonshire and Denbigh Herald*, a paper which was no friend to the Church, reviewing this book, emphasised his bravery. Linking Jones's strictures on the bishop's for their Anglicising policy with David Howell's public row with Bishop Edwards of St Asaph, which also related to these matters of nationality and patriotism, he commented, '[i]f the Bishop of Bangor looks on such matters in the same light as the Bishop of St Asaph, he [Jones] had better bid farewell to promotion, no archdeaconry, prebend, or deanery, will fall to his lot, we are afraid'.[7]

In the same year Jones published an address delivered to the Bangor Diocesan Conference, *Rhwymedigaethau Cenedl y Cymru i'r Eglwys*; it was republished in 1902. The title may be translated as 'The Obligations of the Welsh Nation to the Church', and in it Jones repeated, though by a different and gentler route, the material published in his larger work of that year.

His introduction to this conference address is interesting, however, for here Jones offers some rationale for his historicity. He would differ from most church historians, he asserted, by stating that the hand of God was to be seen as much in the development of the Christian Church as in that of the Jewish or Old Testament Church. God's providential dealings with his people were to be found in the pages of church history, which was therefore to be used as a means of edifying rather than as a matter of debate and controversy. Submitting lock stock and barrel to the Celtic myth, propagated by Bishop Davies – the translator of the New Testament into Welsh – and by Bishop Burgess of St Davids in numerous works, he asserted that the Celtic Church retained the closest relationship of all to the pure Apostolic Church in doctrine and form. It was the last of the churches to be led astray by Popish religion or in submitting to 'the Roman beast' (though he is quoting Bacon here), and even then its submission was never as complete as the English. The Welsh Church, by its marriage to the Church of England, was not thereby any less a Church, while it enabled the Welsh to receive the Scriptures in their own language.

Other sections looked at the Church and Welsh literature, education and almsgiving, but Jones ended with a closing section about the obligations of the Church to the nation. These included a proper humility, the desire to transmit to future generations the ethos of the 'old Welsh Church', purifying and enriching the life of the nation by reminding it of its obligations to God, and being prepared to sacrifice all except truth to do this. The last sentence is significant, for it was written at a time when many men were saying, including Dean Howell, that it might be better to lose 'establishment' and even the Church's endowments if this allowed her to be an indigenous and Gospel Church. Clearly Jones was saying the same thing, though in a more coded message.

In 1902 he published, under the imprint of SPCK, the *Life and Times of Griffith Jones*. Griffith Jones, vicar of Llanddowror, Carmathenshire, was a seminal figure in the life of the eighteenth century nation, who devised the circulating schools which, during his lifetime and beyond, possibly taught at least half the population of Wales to read. His was a spiritual work, designed to promote the well-being of immortal souls and the glory of God, although it had the side-effect of encouraging and stimulating the rise of Methodism. Not only was reading taught, so was psalmody, family prayers and the catechism, spiritual duties were encouraged, and while children were taught by day, adults were taught by night. These schools were a major work of evangelism, and were, as Jones continually pointed out, rooted in the life of the Church. Not surprisingly, Jones used the biography not only to point out the success of this indigenous work, but also to indicate that Griffith Jones's educational work and the church revival it caused helped offset the dead-hand of the Anglo-Welsh episcopate with its Anglicising policy.

But there was more than this to the book. The preface tells another equally valid story. Taking as its theme Griffith Jones's assertion that dissent had been caused by the lack 'of plan, practical, pressing and zealous preaching, in a language and dialect they are able to understand; and freedom of friendly access to advise about their spiritual state', David Jones endeavoured to point out this was as true for Griffith Jones's time as it was for the Methodist secession of 1811. If then, he continued, the Church could show that the original causes of dissent had largely disappeared, for they were practical rather than doctrinal, then the work of reunion should be hastened. As he put it:

> To ponder over its [the book's] lessons in humble earnestness might, under God's blessing, lead to an active desire for Christian reunion on the part of those who are now in a state of separation, and, we fear, sometimes of antagonism. The religious condition of Wales can hardly commend itself to those who are imbued with the spirit of the Intercessory Prayer of Christ; and there is some ground for apprehension lest Welsh Christianity should fail to maintain its efficiency, while it is thus *'a house divided against itself'*. There may be, and doubtless there sometimes has been, a kind of union worse than division; but few will deny that there is a union which, beyond all dispute or comparison, is preferable to disunion.

Jones's formula for unity included an appreciation of the 'loss of power and efficiency incurred by our present anomalous and wasteful condition'; an awareness of the ideal and the practical value of unity; the discernment between the essential aspects of faith and those areas on which Christians could agree to differ; a disposition to emphasise points of agreement rather than of difference, and a spirit of concern for each other. In addition there should be the recognition of that bond of unity which already existed, and a desire for a closer Christian fellowship and communion among all that 'love our Lord Jesus in sincerity'. '[I]ncalculable blessings' would follow such a recognition by the mainstream churches of Wales. As Jones put it, the reunion of Church and Nonconformity could only bring special strengths to the resulting Church:

The freshness and the vigour, the initiative and the elasticity, the sense of the privileges and the responsibilities of the lay members, which the Nonconformists would bring with them, would be an unquestionable gain to the Church of England; while the respect for order and authority, the conservative instinct inherent in so ancient a body as that Church, and the spirit of wise toleration and comprehensiveness which a long experience has taught her, would, if we mistake not, be joyfully welcomed by a large number of thoughtful Nonconformists. Each would, in some degree, supply the deficiencies of the other; and the fusion of the two elements, under favourable conditions, could not fail to strengthen our common Christianity, and to equip it for the more effective discharge of the tremendous responsibilities with which it stands face to face at the present moment.

Consequently, Jones fervently hoped, a consideration of the men and movements depicted in his book would 'soften the asperities of religious life and controversy in Wales, and to work in the direction of reunion'. Reunion would come in God's good time. Jones recognised, however, that such unity was hardly possible in the then temper of the Christian bodies in Wales, even though there were still great duties lying at hand, especially of meeting the growing indifference and irreligion in the land. Nevertheless, Jones proclaimed the need of and the necessity for such unity as could be achieved, in order that a pathway might be established for this work in the future. Let it be remembered, he wrote, that the spiritual revival of Griffith Jones's time came not, 'as some unexpected, unasked-for supernatural manifestation, but in response to the prayers and preparations of faithful men'. Let it be equally remembered that 'spiritual forces are still the most powerful and essential to purify and elevate the life of a people', as was the case during the eighteenth century revival. And let it not be forgotten that human perversities impaired the efficiency of that revival, with the result that the defects in the Church of that day were still being paid for in the disunity and bitterness of their own age. It was a call to prayer and action by clergy and laity alike.[8]

At a time of increased bitterness between the denominations, when Bishop Edwards seemed to be making war upon Nonconformity, and casting scorn upon all those who opposed his policy of retaining the Anglo-Welsh connections and ethos of the Church,[9] David Jones, following the example of David Howell, was longing for a spiritual impetus which would bring about a true and united Church for Wales. It was a bold vision, bolder still for the times in which it was written, and may well have been fuelled by his Nonconformist background.

Jones's last publication, a booklet entitled *The Moral and Religious Condition of Wales, during the last thirty years, on the testimonies of Welsh Nonconformists*, printed at Bangor in 1906, took up this note of concern about the religious state of Wales which he had mentioned in his biography of Griffith Jones. He wrote as a patriot, feeling that a patriot needed to be honest about his country. There had been a loss of belief in the doctrines of the Gospel, he claimed, and this had led to a moral decline. Rather than quote church writers, whose testimony was 'sometimes discounted by the charge that they are too fond of finding fault with Wales', Jones preferred to give the evidence of Nonconformist writers.

Jones also defended himself against those who would argue that the recent Welsh Revival had made obsolete the testimonies he was recording. Yes, he believed that the revival had brought blessings to many, and that it was from God, but the hand of man was too strong for it. As a result it had been used for sectarian and political ends. Consequently, this degrading of 'the holy things of God' had meant that Jesus had 'departed again into a mountain Himself alone', and the revival had subsided within a year. Indeed, Jones's deep concern was that religion and politics had become so mixed up in Wales that truth and spirituality and Christian integrity had been lost. Quoting some of the earlier resolutions of the Welsh Methodists, in addition to John Elias, Lewis Edwards, Henry Richard, and others, Jones showed how they had expressed concern that party politics and religion should be divorced from one another. The failure to do this meant that the churches were being diverted away 'from the one thing needful'. Noting from other writers, including denominational publications, that there had been a decline in the pulpit and in sound doctrine, but an increase in the vanity of preachers, he added their testimony that their congregations' lack of Scripture knowledge allowed these men to get away with deriding the *Confession of Faith* or the old Biblical doctrines of their denominations.

Although Jones did not make the connection between a decline in faith and an increase in immorality as one might have expected, he certainly gave numerous examples of Nonconformist leaders deploring the moral standards of the age. Nevertheless, he made clear that morality had no basis unless it rested upon a religious foundation, and with this in mind the secular education of the Board Schools had been found wanting. Wales was now drifting away from its old religious moorings, and sectarianism had become the blight of Wales. There was more concern for the building up of denominations than about matters of law, truth and justice.

It is interesting that David Jones should have refrained from quoting church sources. His excuse hardly holds water, unless he hoped that his readers would understand that all he said about Nonconformity's sectarianism applied equally to his own

Church and especially to Bishop Edwards's confrontation with Nonconformity. His last section, 'An appeal to Churchmen', certainly hints at this, and deserves to be quoted, though Jones now appears to have withdrawn his desire for unity with Nonconformity. Indeed, he almost suggests that the Church would have to evangelise on its own the large number of people who attended no place of worship at all:

> The message of these pages is primarily to Churchmen. . . . . They will acknowledge that the country's need is the Church's opportunity. Let the Church then gird herself for the task. There is no time to lose. Neither can there be any doubt as to the means which it should employ in its efforts to discharge the duties that lie before it. Churchmen should spare nothing, but cheerfully and ungrudgingly sacrifice everything that is needful to restore to its fold those half a million of souls that have gone astray . . . The weapons for this warfare are none other than *the Gospel of Christ, which is the power of God unto salvation to everyone that believeth*. This should be the Church's answer to-day, while the enemy is at the gate, not in the arrogant spirit that too often characterises the religious controversies of our times, but in the spirit of the meek and lowly Saviour. . . . The sound of menace and of conflict is in the air; formidable obstacles and difficulties of diverse kinds challenge the Church's advance. But these are the tests of its faith – of its belief in the divine origin of its mission. The secret of the Church's strength is not in material resources, or in the number of its adherents, or in the favourable nature of its surroundings, but in the promise and the presence of God. To go in search of the five hundred thousand lost sheep is heaven's clearest call to God's people in Wales.

'God's people in Wales?' Is there not some ambiguity here? At first sight Jones is calling his own Church to an exclusive crusade, but does he mean by that term 'sacrifice' that his own Church might enter into a greater unity for the sake of its mission and perhaps even accept disestablishment for that cause? Perhaps the thought was there, although he had already stated that the disendowment of the Church 'might register a triumph in the annals of mere political warfare, but it would inflict a severe blow on the highest interests of the national life'. The condition of the country called for an increase in resources and opportunities, not for their curtailment. His heart was in the right place, but the task of fulfilling his vision was not an easy one to determine. It is not surprising that he was closely and rather ruthlessly examined on this work by the Royal Commission mentioned earlier. He replied, 'My intention was to rouse my countrymen on the religious side of them to the dangers. I cannot go further than that'.[10]

The bulk of Jones's writing, however, is to be found in the pages of *Y Cyfaill Eglwysig* ('The Church Friend'), which he edited from 1894 until a few months before his death. It is in this monthly publication, of which he is said to have written about half the contents, 15 out of 28 pages, month by month, that the fruits of his diligent reading and his ability to write to purpose are depicted. While meant for children, it had many adult readers, and its context ranged from Biblical and 'Church' articles to matters of general interest. David Howell had commenced its publication in 1862, and although he had written much for it, and appears to have owned the copyright until his death, he never edited it. The paper received a tribute from *Cymro*, a radical Nonconformist paper, that it could not think of a better monthly for its price in Welsh, and it gave high praise to its literary taste.[11]

These writings reveal David Jones to be both an evangelical and a patriot for his nation and Church. His address to the Special Forward Movement of the Church Pastoral-Aid Society – a thoroughly evangelical institution – in 1894 at Exeter Hall, London, clarifies this. A preamble drawing attention to the distinctive character of the Welsh Church, as representing the earliest Christianity in this country, but noting too its poverty, the bitterness of political opposition through the disestablishment campaign, and the indifference and irreligion indicated by a moral collapse and the half million non-church goers, led him to call for 'redoubled efforts on behalf of the Church'.

It was a tragedy, he argued, to handicap religion by disendowment 'at the moment when the battle promises to be most severe'. It was not a moment too soon to enter upon a forward movement. The fields were ripe for harvest, but men of the right stamp were needed, men of natural ability, consecrated by the Holy Ghost, trained by experience, devoted to their work. A theological college was needed to train them. The movement needed to be loyal to Church and Reformation principles, which meant confidence in the Prayer Book, the Creeds, Articles, Homilies, Sacraments and Orders, and 'in our liberty and independence'. Without that confidence in 'the truths we are pledged to preach and maintain' it would neither impress men nor 'bring down the blessing of God upon our Church and country'.

Wales, Jones claimed, was ripe for such an aggressive movement and would respond to it, being weary of 'contending factions, of jarring discords and controversies'. Above all it must be a spiritual movement, and party spirit and antipathies must be kept out of it. But it needed to be on the line of evangelical principles, 'not because there is a party which calls itself Evangelical, but because we believe those truths, those principles, are the only ones which can deal successfully with the rationalism, the scepticism, and the irreligion which the Forward Movement proposes to touch'. The old evangelical movement was not dead, nor was it dying, but its powers needed to be multiplied a hundredfold, and to this end Jones urged his hearers to sacrifice and prayer.[12]

Speaking to a specifically north Wales meeting of this

Society, designed to strengthen the evangelical cause amongst Welsh clergymen, in that same year, Jones argued the need for strengthening the links between evangelical clergy and laity in order to assert 'our doctrinal and ritual position as Churchmen', and to enable English evangelicals to understand the position in Wales. They were living in an age when the air was full of sacerdotalism, and the ritualistic party was well organised and united. By contrast to this fashionable trend, 'Evangelicalism is tabooed. If we are quiet and acquiescent we are tolerated; but if we assert our position and claim our rights we are called bigoted and self-seeking'. It was becoming an age of spiritual indifference, while many educated Nonconformists were giving more attention to political matters than to spiritual concerns. But Wales was still a favourable field for the growth of evangelical principles. Whilst fashionable, sacerdotalism and rationalism were confined to a few, but the bulk of the population – especially the Welsh-speaking part – were still 'sound to the core', and a plain evangelical discourse which centred on the themes of the Incarnation, the Atonement and the Person of the Holy Spirit was popular with them. The stability of the Church in Wales depended upon an evangelical ministry, especially as its 'soil' was congenial to its growth. This was because 'the arrogant and exclusive claims of the sacerdotalist party' had embittered the people of Wales against the Church. Sacerdotalism had led many Nonconformists into believing that the Church should be disestablished. Church defence needed to be carried out on national and evangelical grounds, and would then be 'in a position to defy all assaults and all assailants'.

Jones's plea to this conference of evangelical clergymen, therefore, was for greater unity and co-operation amongst Church evangelicals in Wales; further and public efforts to support the Church Pastoral-Aid Society and the Church Missionary Society as evangelical institutions; an annual conference for evangelical clergy, and the revival of preaching meetings. The Church was nowhere so strong as it was in those places where these preaching meetings had been held, such as Cardiganshire, while 'the prayerful cultivation of this divine institution' would encourage Christians and help maintain good standards of preaching.[13]

We return to David Jones's main work, *The Welsh Church and Welsh Nationality*, bearing in mind the various lines of thought Jones had already given us in his other works. Its main argument may be illustrated by this extract from his introduction:

I maintain that the Anglicising policy does not represent the wisest and justest administrative principles of the Welsh Church, and that the advanced section of Welsh politicians do not reflect the truest political instincts and traditions of the Welsh nation. In the following pages, an attempt is made to show how history bears out the first part of this proposition; and if leisure is afforded me, I hope, ere long, to prove the second part, by showing how great and how numerous have been the benefits which the Welsh Church has, through a course of many centuries, conferred on the Welsh nation, how identical their interests have been, and how their present partial separation was brought about, not through any conviction on the part of those who left her of the unscripturalness of the doctrine or the polity of the Church, nor through any revolt against her position, but chiefly through the folly and injustice of the policy illustrated and condemned in these pages.

Here he was following Dean Edwards. But his was a plea for moderation which owed much to Dean Howell's writings:

These are the days of unrest . . . Controversy is doing deadly injury to the highest interests of the Principality. Combatants are raising spirits from 'the vasty deep' which are no less fatal to themselves than to their opponents. Words are uttered and written that are as poisoned daggers plunged into the vitals of Christianity. Victory won by marching over the prostate form of spiritual religion, would be the defeat of everything that has made Wales what she is to-day, and is capable of raising her still to higher elevations. The first care of every Christian patriot should be to avert this defeat. In the sharp conflict of opinions and strife of tongues that now disturb and distract an impulsive race, it should ever be remembered that infinitely more precious blessings are imperilled by the controversy than the mere temporal possessions around which it rages, even the blessings of charity, and peace and good will, which nothing is more calculated to blight than polemical bitterness, and the heated atmosphere of political partisanship and for the loss of which, no possible triumph that either side may gain, can ever bring adequate compensation, either to itself or to the country. The great need of Wales to-day is men of 'light and leading', whose vision is clear enough to discern the magnitude of the interests that are at stake, and whose voice is authoritative enough to restore to the nation, calmness of belief – strength and stability of conviction – men whose individual gifts and character can afford to dispense with the coarse weapons of party tactics and recriminations, and, free from the taint of vulgar ambition, can appeal to the masses from the ground of Christian patriotism. I have confidence in the generosity of my countrymen, that such men would not appeal to them in vain.

It is quite clear from these extracts, as it is from all Jones's writings, that the moderate policies of Howell and his friends were being commended, and the polemical and controversial policies of Bishop Edwards and his group condemned. Their policy was one of estranging the Welsh Church from the nation by continuing an Anglicising policy, while another group, mainly Nonconformists and politicians, wished to strip the Church of all her influence and possessions. But there was a third policy, supported by a large number of the Welsh clergy and the vast majority of the Welsh Church laity: '[t]heirs is the policy of working the Welsh Church on Welsh lines, with due regard to the indelible characteristics and the legitimate aspirations of the Welsh people.' Those who had advocated and practised this policy for many centuries had ensured that there was still a remnant of the Welsh-speaking people 'zealously attached to the Church of their forefathers', and the highest hopes of the Welsh Church depended on the success of this policy.

The history of the Church in Wales showed that this Anglicising policy had gained strength since the late seventeenth century, Jones asserted. Before that date Wales was 'most Welsh' when it was identified with the Church. Following A. J. Johnes's book on the reasons for Welsh dissent, Jones went onto to suggest that there had been a sustained attempt to erase the Welsh language, to identify it with Nonconformity, and to make its language appear a vulgar and peasant affair. This was a policy which resulted in an attempt to depreciate the Welsh clergy by denying them the higher appointments of the Church; which introduced English-speaking clergy into Welsh parishes, and endeavoured to deny the natural unity of Wales. The Church which had retained and enhanced the Welsh language in the past was now pouring scorn upon it as a result of this policy. A spirit had been created which had not only marginalised the language but had also exhibited a want of sympathy with Welsh feeling and spirituality. The result had been that the Church had become an alien body and the Welsh people had drifted into Nonconformity. Yet it was the inferior Welsh clergy who were winning their way among the Welsh masses, being more sympathetic with the genius, national temperament, and characteristics of the people. If authority and power still came from above, 'popular influence and reform have hitherto come from below'.

The difficulties of the Church had not been caused by poverty, Jones claimed, for where the Church was wealthiest, there she was at her weakest. Rather the poverty-stricken Welsh clergy had kept alive 'the fire on her altars for a miserable pittance', and the native heart of the Church 'still beats in harmony with the noblest aspirations of the Cymry, and her right hand is full of gifts to bless and to elevate them'. What she had done in the past, in being the spiritual heart of a nation, she could do again, but to do so the policy needed to be changed, and leaders appointed who were in sympathy with the aspirations and desires of a fervent people. Let the Church 'approach her lost children in her older spirit, and her older love, and she will find that they are still the same warm-hearted, loyal, trustful people as when they drank unitedly at her wells of the water of life, and shared her destiny in shadow and sunshine'. A church, like a nation which renounces its past, also renounces its future, he concluded.

But how far was this the writing of a 'Welsh Anglican reactionary', to quote Emlyn Sherrington's phrase? How far was Jones influenced by those who felt that Anglicanism needed to be defeated in the Church and the Welsh Church separated from Canterbury on nationalistic grounds, or felt that the 'New Liberalism' so far from being a moral crusade of high principle, was a naked grab for power 'by a self-seeking, abrasive middle class' who wished 'to keep the Bible out of schools . . . and turn Churchmen out of their Churches'? How far did he feel that the principles of this group were a perpetuation of the poison which had 'all but ruined Europe since 1789'? Or did David Jones simply long for a non-political nationalism, when the nation would be led by men whose sole concern was the welfare of the nation and the good of the Church rather than for any ulterior purpose?

It is hard to say. Certainly Jones expressed concern about the state of morality and religion in his day. Undoubtedly others such as Wade-Evans and de Hirsch-Davies elaborated his theories and extended his arguments. But Jones made it clear he had no wish of 'assuming an organised existence apart from the great English Church; nor does the Welsh nation, if I am not greatly mistaken, entertain the least desire of severing its destinies from the great English people', even though 'such dreams may occasionally flit across the disordered brains of a few enthusiasts'.[14]

David Jones never put his thoughts into a coherent and well-ordered shape. Possibly he died before he could do so. But his writings, polemical though they may be, urged a gentle moderation, a quiet godly work, and a change in the policy of the Church which respected the Welsh nation instead of working against the upthrust of the patriotism of his own day. He deplored the introduction of party politics into religious affairs, and longed for his Church to be at the centre of the nation's life, uniting all its spiritual people into one, restoring it to a sense of godliness and hope, and enabling it to be a light to the wider society in which it lived. His dream may not have been articulated in a formal sense, but surely that was his desire. David Jones was a prophet, and has received the usual prophet's reward.[15]

ENDNOTES

1 Emlyn Sherrington, 'Welsh Nationalism, the French Revolution, and the Influence of the French Right 1880-1930', in David Smith (ed), *A People and a Proletariat* (London, 1980), p. 145.
2 *Y Cyfaill Eglwysig*, 1909, pp. 169-74, 255-7.
3 D. G. Osborne-Jones, *Edward Richard of Ystradmeurig* (Carmarthen, 1934), pp. 157-60.
4 *Report of the Royal Commission on the Church of England and other Religious Bodies in Wales* (London, 1911), III 90-101; *Y Cyfaill Eglwysig*, pp. 172-4; *Record*, 2 September 1898, p. 851. His ordination papers, in the Church in Wales records at the NLW (B/O/1128) of 18 December 1875 reveal that his letters testimonial were signed by three Cardiganshire incumbents,

including Dean Lewellin of Lampeter.

5 *Y Cyfaill Eglwysig*, p. 171; Morfudd Jones, *The History of St Cadwaladr's Church, Llangadwaladr* (1986), p. 18.

6 *Report*, III 95; David Jones (ed), *Wales and the Welsh Church* (London, 1889), pp. 45, 52-7, 61f, 70f, 83f, 90-3.

7 David Jones, *The Welsh Church and Welsh Nationality* (London, 1893), pp. viiif; *Caernarvonshire and Denbigh Herald*, 21 July 1893, p. 4; *Record*, 28 July 1893, p. 723.

8 David Jones, *Life and Times of Griffith Jones* (London, 1902), pp. vii-xvi. No single work has yet replaced this biography, in spite of its obvious defects.

9 For a background to this controversy see my article, 'Traitors and Compromisers: The Shadow Side of the Church's Fight against Disestablishment', in *Journal of Welsh Religious History*, 3 (1995) 35-53, and my biography of David Howell (Denbigh, 1998), pp. 157-86, 195-7, 211-36.

10 David Jones, *The Moral and Spiritual Condition of Wales* (Bangor, 1906), in passim, but the quotations are from pp. 56 and 61f; *Report*, III 96f. An article by David Jones on the revival appeared in the *Record* (31 March 1905, pp. 301-2). Accepting its divine origin, and as being God's gift to the nation, Jones was encouraged that the bishops and leaders, as well as the clergy and laity of the Church, had welcomed it. This was far different from the attitude in 1859, the previous revival, and Jones attributed this to the fact that a number of north Wales clergy had agreed to pray between seven and nine in the morning for a greater manifestationof the Holy Spirit in the life of the Church. Archdeacon Hugh Jones and Dean Howell had been amongst the pioneers of this movement in 1886. Such a revival was sorely needed, and there was no doubt that the fruits of the spirit were being manifested by it; debts had been paid, quarrels settled, services filled, drunkards brought to sobriety, and a spiritual joy and desire filled the lives of converts. Amongst them were a group of toughs from his own parish. After the first two had been converted, they joined together to pray for their colleagues, and now all but one had joined them. The clergy testified that not only were the services better attended and more fervent, but also that the people were not only willing but eager to take part in church work and in prayer meetings. But, he added, the Revival had powerful adverse forces to contend with. The young, chiefly affected by it, showed signs of wishing to be independent of the older people and the religious leaders, though this was not so true of the Church, while the political spirit and sectarian narrowness 'so prevalent in Wales are also a serious hindrance to the spirit of true Revival'.

11 *Y Cyfaill Eglwysig*, p. 173; *Report*, pp. 93, 100. J. Morgan Gibbon tried his best to suggest that this periodical should be described as 'denominational – Anglican; political – Conservative', which Jones denied.

12 *Church and People* (Church Pastoral-Aid Society), 6 (1895), pp. 229f. It was entitled 'The Church in Wales; its needs and its hopes'.

13 Ibid, pp. 161-3. One of his remarks characterises his style, and perhaps his prejudices: 'Until then (ten years ago) *Gwyddel o babydd* – an Irish Roman

Catholic – in the estimation of Welshman was synonymous with the most abandoned and bloodthirsty miscreant. To-day he is looked upon as an enlightened fellow-citizen and an invaluable political ally.' (p. 162).

14 Jones, *Welsh Church and Welsh Nationality*, in passim, but especially pp. ix-xi, xviii-xx, 8, 113-7; Sherrington, 'Welsh Nationalism', pp. 129-31, 138; *Record*, 28 July 1893, p. 723. For Dean Howell's thoughts on this subject see my biography of David Howell, pp. 171-2, 175-81.

15 David Jones died after a long illness on 2 June 1909, aged 61. He had hoped to go to the continent in order to convalescence, but his condition did not allow it. He left a wife and two children, Dafydd and Mari.

PARSON BY THE COPPERWORKS
The Revd M. Rice Morgan of Llansamlet

Morgan Rice Morgan was appointed by Bishop Thirlwall of St David's to the perpetual curacy of Llansamlet in 1842, having served as curate of the parish since 1833. Its then vicar, Henry Howell Griffiths, was an absentee incumbent but not a pluralist, as he held no other living. Morgan was to write later that Griffiths had had to leave the parish some years earlier as the copper-smoke had injured his health. In one sense Morgan was the first 'vicar' of Llansamlet, for he had been originally appointed as its perpetual curate by the bishop's licence, and thus could be removed from the parish by its withdrawal. However, on pointing out to the Ecclesiastical Commissioners that he held the vicarial tithes of the parish, his request to be made 'vicar' under the District Church Tithes Act of 1865 was allowed, and this gave Morgan security of tenure – the so-called 'parson's freehold'. In addition Morgan held in plurality, and by licence of the archbishop of Canterbury, the adjoining parish of St John's Swansea. The churches were within three miles of one other. His small, neat, distinct handwriting, cramming the paper from edge to edge, remained the same for most of his life, together with the motto on his letterheads, *Ein Hiaith a'n Heglwys* – our Language and Church. Morgan was very much a Welshman, and this neat cramped style of writing was rather indicative of his character.

Llansamlet had always been a poor parish, and until the late eighteenth century its small population consisted of tenant farmers and their labourers. It is not surprising that it was held in plurality from the sixteenth century onwards with another parish, with one brief exception during the earlier years of the nineteenth century. For most of this time the parish had been held in plurality with the neighbouring parish of Llangyfelach, which was also in the patronage of the bishop of St David's. By the late eighteenth century, however, the industrial developments in the northern part of Swansea had brought a huge influx of people into these two parishes. As a result Bishop Burgess ended this plurality in 1805, appointing Evan Lloyd to Llangyfelach. Although Lloyd was an absentee he continued to hold the living for many years. In 1842 Llangyfelach had an income of £159 and a population of 7,753, while Llansamlet had an income of £150 and a population of 3,137.

We can trace some of this history from the returns made by the various perpetual curates of Llansamlet to Queen Anne's Bounty. Llansamlet, being a poor parish, benefited considerably from its funds. In 1754, John Price, its perpetual curate, in answer to queries designed to ensure that his parish was qualified to receive a 'lot' of £200, replied that his income was a mere £12 per annum from this parish, which he described as neither rectory nor vicarage but as an impropriate curacy. He also returned that he had been collated to the neighbouring parish of Llangyfelach, whose income gave him another £13 per annum. A note pencilled into the margin of this return by some Bounty official indicates that these two parishes had been held together since the time of 'Henry VIII'. Charles Harris, incumbent in 1791, answering another enquiry, stated that he was obliged to employ a curate to do duty for him at Llansamlet. This curate was Benjamin Davies, who performed a Welsh service at 9.30 a.m. on Sundays and an English service at noon. The status of these parishes still caused confusion, and Harris merely added to that confusion by arguing that they did not form a consolidated parish, but rather that the same person was generally presented to both. In 1824, Henry Howell Griffiths, who had been offered the living of Llansamlet by the bishop, asked the governors of the Bounty if they could augment his poor living. He was told that the bishop had not certified the living to them, that is, declared its value, but if he remedied this there was a real possibility that it could be augmented as its value was only £60 though its population was over 3,000.

The subsequent enquiry revealed that the population had been over-estimated. It was 2,639, and the income was £76 gross and £63 net. This income came from a variety of sources. The tithes brought in £49 and the rent of land purchased with the various Bounty 'lots' gave another £20. A subsequent letter revealed that this tithe income was decreasing because of 'the destructive effect of the copper works on all the products of the soil'. This was a story that would be endlessly repeated in future years, and which forms the background to Rice Morgan's ministry in this parish.

As a result of this request and enquiry the living of Llansamlet was augmented by a grant of £1,000, which was given from funds provided by Parliament towards the work of QAB. Griffiths wrote a letter in reply which must have pleased the governors: 'I assure you that it will be my study to evince my gratitude for your kindness by a zealous attention to the important duties of my situation.' This grant allowed an annual payment of £40. Further help came some years later. The former bishop of St David's, Thomas Burgess, gave £200 to the benefice as an augmentation during 1827-8, and this was met by an equal grant of the same amount by the governors. At first the governors thought that the bishop's gift was for the living of Llangyfelach, but the registrar of the diocese, Charles Morgan of Carmarthen, queried this on 5 December 1827. He had heard, he wrote, the bishop mentioning Llansamlet in connection with this grant, not Llangyfelach. The former was a small perpetual curacy, but the latter a rich vicarage. As Llangyfelach with its £150 per annum could hardly be described in such terms, Morgan may have been more concerned that its incumbent, Mr

Lloyd, was an absentee, for he pointedly declared that he did not reside in his parish but at East Tilbury, Essex.

A parliamentary enquiry took place in 1832 into the revenues and resources of the Established Church, preparatory to the formation of the Ecclesiastical Commission. Henry Howell Griffiths responded for his parish of Llansamlet. Its population, he returned, was 3,187, the church had accommodation for 400 people, and he undertook the duty each Sunday morning. There was no vicarage house and he had to pay £12 per annum for lodgings out of a gross income of £112. His income was much the same as that returned earlier to the Bounty governors, save that the tithe income had decreased to £39. His was a declining income, he wrote, and he anticipated that it would decline from three to five pounds each year on account of the injurious qualities of the copper smoke which was gradually destroying the vegetation in that part of his parish. His successor was to wax even more eloquently on this subject.

But there were two strokes of luck in the 1840s. One of the first acts of the new Ecclesiastical Commission in Wales was to give a grant of £24 per annum to the living of Llansamlet in order to bring up its stipend to £150 per annum. This was in 1841. It was a much needed gesture and one anticipates that it was given in order to ensure that Llansamlet would not be held in plurality with another parish. This, however, did not happen as we note later. The second stroke of luck came soon afterwards.

In 1821, the then incumbent, Daniel Rowlands, had used the QAB grants given to the parish between 1755-92, amounting to £800 in all, to purchase two fields comprising ten acres of land in the parish of St Peter's Carmarthen.[1] During the 1840s these fields were chosen as the site for the new church training college for schoolmasters at Carmarthen, later to be known as Trinity College. Bishop Thirlwall, much involved in this new college, requested Rice Morgan (now pepetual curate) to sell them for this purpose. He was not unwilling, especially as he believed he could obtain a better rate from this investment than its agricultural rental of £25 per annum. In any case it would be to his advantage to sell a glebe at some considerable distance from his parish and on which dilapidations had to be assessed and paid. In fact he received the sum of £905 from this sale, which added to various other sums held by the Bounty on behalf of the parish of £112, allowed him an additional annual income of £34. But Morgan was rather put out that the foundation stone of the college had been laid before the legal formalities had been completed. He also, characteristically, insisted that the college authorities pay all the legal expenses of the conveyance, refusing to allow a sum of £30 to be deducted from the sale price for this purpose.

****

Though Morgan had to cope with immense problems in his parish, it is clear that he was a conscientious pastor. He was instumental in building up large congregations and was deeply concerned about extending the Church's influence throughout his parish. This emerges in two letters he wrote to QAB. Writing on 19 April 1862 to its governors, Rice Morgan stated that he had built a new church in the parish almost as soon as he became its incumbent, and this church now had over 300 communicants. Morgan was referring to the chapel of ease which had been built at Kilvey. It served the Foxhole area of his parish. Four years later in a letter to the commissioners [9 April 1866] he extended this statement, but now he was a little more realistic. He had built a beautiful new church for the workmen of the copperworks which had cost £2,000 to £3,000. (In fact, much of the credit for its building probably lay with a local industrialist, Pascoe Grenfell.) His curate was labouring hard in that district, taking three services per week, and caring for the 200 communicant members he had brought together.[2] Morgan's letter of 1862 had also referred to his own work at the parish church. There had been a considerable increase in the number of worshippers and during the previous three weeks he had received no less than 40 new members. There were now five services in the parish every Sunday, two in the parish church, the one at 11.00 a.m. being an English service and the evening one at 6.00 p.m. being the Welsh service. These times had replaced the double duty of 10.30 a.m. and 3.00 p.m. which Morgan had introduced when he came into the parish, for previously there had only been a single Sunday service. There were also cottage lectures and weekday services. In 1847 Morgan had given evidence to the celebrated government enquiry into the state of education in Wales. Its report became known in some circles as *The Treachery of the Blue Books*. Morgan informed the local commissioner that he had established a schoolroom in the parish in 1841 under the auspices of Mrs Bevan's Charity, and this had been continued by means of a deduction made from the workmen's wages. By 1848 a site had been granted for a National School. He also added to this enquiry that he did not find the people of Llansamlet particularly ignorant as he went about his clerical visits. Rather, they had had good parish priests in the past and were considered to be 'religious'.[3]

****

We have already noted the various comments made about the smoke from the copper works, its direct effect on the fertility of the soil, and its indirect effect on the tithe income of the parish. Confirmation of this is found in a number of mid-nineteenth century reports. One is the report of the 1847 commissioners into education in Wales, which reported of Llansamlet:

From the sea upwards to Morriston there is a succession of enormous copper-works. There is not a blade of vegetation to be seen on the steep hills of either side of the river, which seem to have been greatly raised, if not in some places created, by accumulations of slag. This, with the whitish smoke of the furnaces, and the penetrating taste of copper, makes the whole region as dreary and disagreeable as I can imagine any to be.[4]

Another description of this area is contained in a series of reports on the manufacturing areas of Great Britain which appeared in the *Morning Chronicle*. It gave this description of the copper industry in Swansea:

The first and most disagreeable sensation which the visitor experiences on entering copper-works is an irritability of the lungs, occasioned by the white sulphurous smoke he necessarily breathes. This smoke in some if not in all states of the atmosphere, is heavier than air, and descends to the ground. On the morning that I visited Havod-works, it hung low – magnifying the men and horses at the canal in the same manner as a wet fog does, and concealing the deadly effect this smoke has upon vegetation, and the singular diseases it occasions in cattle, horses, and sheep.[5]

Writing to the commissioners in May 1843 Morgan maintained that the Haford Works was the largest copperworks in the world, and that his particular case was unique. Unfortunately these works were situated in the area from which he obtained his tithes. A commission of 1853, appointed to investigate the circumstances of the parish as Morgan was endeavouring to obtain a grant for the building of a parsonage house, reported that much of the land was now worthless as its surface had been destroyed by the poisonous effect of this smoke. In 1843 Morgan claimed he had been offered only £58 by the tithe payers whereas the tithe had once been worth over £98, and in

July 1853 he stated that he had been forced to commute his tithes at £46 instead of the £90 he would have received if the farms had not been neglected. A later letter to the commissioners of July 1862 claimed that these tithes should have been worth £120, but Morgan's exactitude in financial matters was generally more optimistic than realistic. Furthermore the landlords refused to pay, with the result that he had had to suffer an increasing loss year by year. In April 1866 he informed the commissioners that Lord Jersey's agent had told him that if he could find anything on the land he was welcome to it. He was now losing £10 to £15 per annum on the value of the tithe while the land belonging to the benefice would soon be a barren and deserted wilderness. Were he to fight for his rights in the courts he would be involved in even greater difficulties. Even though he did not receive anything like the full value of the commuted tithe, he was still required to pay rates and taxes amounting to £15 per annum based on its theoretical rather than its actual value. The landlords, although they had lost these lands as agricultural tenancies, had been able to lease the mineral rights, and so obtained a first rate harvest from them in another way. As his income declined theirs increased.

In 1843 (two years after he had been appointed incumbent), Morgan described the circumstances of his parish to the commissioners. He noted that the Llangyfelach tithes had been commuted at the sum of 1,000 guineas of which the major share of £800 had gone to the commissioners as forming part of the estate of the bishop of St David's. Claiming that this parish had been consolidated with his own parish, he asked whether the commissioners might assist him with a local claim based upon this tithe income in order that he could more amply provide for the spiritual necessities of his poor parishioners. As his own tithe income had fallen, perhaps the commissioners could make up his income by £25 to the £150 which they had certified as the value of the living two years previously? The forms for that grant, he now suggested, had been filled up by an absentee incumbent who was not aware of the real circumstances of his parish, with the result that he had given the living a higher value than was justified. Besides this, the parochial fees had been much diminished as the 'sectarians' were now able to marry in their own dissenting chapels, and in such a populous parish as his this made a great difference to the surplice fees. The men of property had moved away. Their seats were now desolate. But he remained, for

> [t]he poor clergyman cannot, dare not turn away but he is obliged to be at his post, endeavouring to instruct the thousands of poor colliers and the ignorant coppermen who are committed to his charge, in their duty towards God and their neighbour, looking for his reward and remuneration in the world to come.

Unpleasant as the smoke was, Morgan claimed he would be quite content to remain and labour amongst his parishioners, who consisted of colliers, miners, labourers, coppermen and small farmers, if his income could be augmented to £150 per annum. Mercifully the commissioners ensured that his reward for living in his smoke-filled habitation did not have to wait for another world for he received what he requested. Another £15 was added on to their augmentation, and this was gazetted in April 1844. The income was now made up from such sums as the income arising from the selling of the glebe £35, the various augmentations made by the Bounty and the Commissioners of £85, £15 in fees, and £38 from the tithe income, less deductions.

****

When Morgan arrived in the parish there was no glebe or parsonage house available; in fact he claimed to be the first resident incumbent for many years. Neither was there any house suitable as a parsonage available for rent within the parish. The only convenient house available, just outside the parish, was at Penywern, Swansea, and this he rented at a cost of £15 per annum. During the 1850s Morgan determined to remedy this position and build his own vicarage for, as he wrote to the governors on 25 July 1853, it was essential that a suitable house of residence should be provided.

The first necessity was a site. Luckily Morgan managed to persuade Lord Jersey, the local landowner, to present him with a site next to the parish church. It was a good site, a capital place, a lovely spot, and convenient to the church, he informed the governors of the Bounty on 10 June 1853, and it was valued at between £100 and £150. But if he had had to fight hard to obtain this land, Morgan was going to have to fight even harder to have a parsonage house built on this site. From the start Morgan made it clear that he did not expect to have to offer any money of his own for this undertaking, writing: 'it can hardly be expected that I should lay out any money of my own upon premises which may be occupied and in the possession of another even before I should go to enjoy it, even if I had money to spare, which I am sorry to say is not the case.' In the same letter he made it clear that he hoped the governors would pay all the legal costs involved in the transfer of the land, and that the commissioners should compensate him for the loss of fees at his district church. They did neither. After much bargaining the governors allowed him to use up to £500 capital from the sale of the former glebe land. Although this would decrease his income correspondingly, the amount he would lose was probably equivalent to the rental of an alternative house. He was also successful in obtaining a grant of £200 from the Gally Knight Fund held by the commissioners for the building of parsonages.

The architect, David Jones of Swansea, drew up the plans. They originally comprised a central staircase with dining and drawing rooms to the left and a study to the right, with the kitchen offices aside and a stable adjoining. There were five bedrooms on the first floor, together with a servants' staircase. A cesspool lay within yards of the kitchen wall. Both the governors and the commissioners required these plans to be inspected and approved by their own architects as a condition of the grants, and while it appears the Bounty architect merely queried some of the arrangements, the commissioners' architect declined to accept them. The rooms were too small, the largest reception room was but 14 by 13 feet, the best bedroom was only 10 feet wide, and too much space was wasted on corridors and a second staircase. The water supply and the sanitary fittings were totally deficient. The plans should either be modified or better still redrawn.

Writing to the governors of the Bounty on 23 May 1853 Morgan replied to their architect's queries. They were quite correct: there was no water supply to the house. This was because the house was set on a 'pretty little hill' and so it would be far too expensive to take water up to it. Instead there was a well of water 300 yards away at the bottom of the hill and on the parish road. This water was common property and all the villagers obtained their supply from it. He might have added that servants were cheap in those days as well. This was also the reason why there was no water closet. It would be absurd to have a water closet without a plentiful supply of water and to provide a space for this on the first floor would cost an additional £20. Anyrate, a double privy had been provided in the garden. One side was for the family. The other for the servants. The second staircase was essential, Morgan argued. It was far more important than a water closet. He had never had a house without such a staircase. Clearly servants were not only to be carriers of water but also unseen in this household! But he did not understand what the governors meant by a lack of fittings. His friends were astonished by how much could be done for so small a sum, though he accepted that he himself would have to provide grates and bookshelves, and plant the garden, for these were matters additional to the contract. These items, which also included a cistern, kitchen dressers and a pigsty, would cost another £127.

Morgan had assumed all along that the governors of the Bounty would accept Lord Jersey's gift of land for the vicarage site as a benefaction and meet it with an equal grant. Their refusal came as a great shock. In all he had £700 available; the £500 allowed him from the sale of the glebe and the £200 grant from the Gally Knight Fund. The cost of the house, as originally planned, was estimated at £627. But this was before the commissioners' architect had made his report and increased the costs considerably. But even the estimates based on this new plan proved woefully inadequate, for the actual cost of this 'new-style' house turned out to be £1,300. In further letters, written after the house had been built, Morgan wrote that he not realised the implications of accepting this Gally Knight grant. It had meant that the commissioners had become actively involved in the building, demanding substantial alterations to the plans which had resulted in a near doubling of the cost of the building. When he had realised this the work was in progress and it was too late to withdraw. The commissioners' rules and regulations had cost him an additional £400 to £500, and all this for the sake of a grant of £200. The Bounty's architect, he pointed out, was quite satisfied with his plans. Even Bishop Thirlwall, who was not particularly sympathetic to Morgan, as we note later, conceded the justice of his assertions. Morgan nursed his wrath for many years.

But as in all house building, problems soon appeared.

There had been a considerable delay in the conveying of the site of the vicarage to the commissioners by the solicitors of Lord Jersey. Until the site had been conveyed no grants could be paid, and until the grants were available no work could commence. This was because the builder was paid in instalments for work certified by the architect from monies allowed by the Bounty or granted through the commissioners, but which they retained in their own hands. By June 1853 Morgan was becoming desperate and wrote to Christopher Hodgson, the Bounty's secretary, asking that he should 'plead' for him, 'a poor clergyman' whose parish had not been blessed with a resident clergyman for many years. The weather suitable for building was coming to a close, yet everything was ready for work to commence. This matter was eventually sorted out.

The second matter has already been noted, the substantial and unexpected additional costs of the building. The builder had estimated the revised plans at £853, upon which the governors allowed Morgan to draw a further £128 of the glebe sale money. Thomas Morris, the contractor, duly signed the necessary papers declaring that he would build a house to the specifications provided for the sum he had estimated, and not require any additional sums from either of the two financing agencies. But, in a letter expressing some panic and dated 11 September 1854, Morgan wrote to the governors stating that five months ago he believed all was well, but now both builder and architect had told him they had completely miscalculated their costings and could not build the house for the sum stipulated. The builder claimed that his figures were based on the costings in force when his estimate had been given, but during the long delay wages had increased and the building materials were costing more than he had anticipated. They were at least £200 short. It was pointless proceeding against the contractor, wrote Morgan, and sending him to gaol would solve nothing. The man believed himself to be totally ruined, and he had charged nothing for himself beyond his bare wages. His good friend, the vicar of Swansea, Edward Squire, had been in the same position recently. But the whole situation was disturbing his peace of mind. His nights were sleepless and he felt that he would have to abandon the whole work, for it was clear that the builder could not complete the work without incurring additional costs.

A further letter was delivered to the governors during the

course of the next month. Written from Llanelli Vicarage, where Morgan was staying in order to recover his health, he wrote that he had seen Bishop Thirlwall, and he had followed the bishop's advice and had applied for a grant to Marshall's Trustees. But the additional costs had now risen to £335. It seems they rose even higher, and although Morgan was not successful in his application to this trust, possibly because work had already started, the governors of the Bounty now allowed him to draw on the full amount (£992) of the funds held in trust for his parish. However, Morgan never forgot that he had had to find £150 out of his own pocket in order to complete the house, which he claimed had impoverished his family. Furthermore, the loss of such a substantial sum as £992 from the capital of the living had diminished his annual income by at least £30, while he considered that the house he had been forced to build by the commissioners was more suited to a person with a stipend of £500 than to one with £150, for its upkeep cost him between £30 to £35 a year.

From the time of his earliest application Morgan had made clear that he needed outhouses, such as a cowhouse, barn, coach house and stables, at a cost of at least £100, together with the walling of the grounds. But this work had to wait for a number of years after the completion of the house. Writing to the governors in February 1862 Morgan noted that he had been labouring in the parish since 1833 under many disadvantages. He had a large family to support and educate. In addition there had been all the problems associated with the building of the vicarage which had forced him to find £150 out of his own limited resources. He was only able to complete the house by neglecting this work of walling the property and building the outhouses. The result was that while the house was placed in the middle of land owned by Lady Jersey he had never been able to fence it or form a garden or pleasure ground. The cost of this would be at least £200. He was unable to lay this amount out himself because of the expenditure on the house. Yet it was essential that this was done, for the place was in a shocking state, and was not only causing him and his family much inconvenience, but also embarrassment when people called. The work needed to be done for a clergyman to live there with any degree of comfort.

The bishop of St David's, Morgan understood, was prepared to give a grant of £200 from his funds, but he was only able to do so if it could be met by a grant from another source. The additional grant, he made clear, would form an augmentation for the living, helping to replace the income lost through the building of the house. His income was now only £149 10s. gross, and allowing for the tithe income loss of £5 10s, collecting expenses of £3 10s. and other expenses, it was barely £118 net. By this date, however, Morgan clearly felt he had to mention the circumstances of his plurality, for such matters were becoming a matter of some distaste to church reformers. Yes, he held the living of St John's, he wrote, but his successor would not be able to do so because of the change in the law. He would thus be reduced to living on an income of only £118. And this was totally insufficient for such a parish as Llansamlet. His parishioners were all working people, and he had no resident landowners or proprietors to assist his work, yet while his income was declining because of the decrease in the tithe, the population of his parish was increasing.

This letter was not only an appeal, it was also a defence. For in the course of what he described as a 'long and rather unpleasant' correspondence with his bishop about that anticipated grant, Bishop Thirlwall had accused him of building a house greater than his resources. Although the bishop later retracted this accusation, he was clearly annoyed that Morgan was being a little economical with the truth so far as the grant was concerned.

Eventually the governors allowed him a grant of £100 to meet this episcopal benefaction of £200, but this made Morgan rather disgruntled, for he had expected it to be equal to the benefaction. At the same time, May 1862, he endeavoured to persuade the governors to invest what remained of his money in the Swansea Harbour Trust, which paid a five per cent interest rate compared to the three and a quarter per cent paid by the Bounty office. He was equally annoyed by the governors' 'misconception' that he wanted both the benefaction and the grant money to be used for his improvements. Rather, he wrote, he wanted the £200 benefaction to be used to augment the value of his living, although how he anticipated he could complete the outhouses and the walling of the grounds for £100 was never explained. A letter of 16 June 1862 ended with words which clearly indicated his disillusionment; as the clergy could not help themselves we 'must suffer ourselves to receive what is granted to us by those in higher powers, to be taxed and rated and assessed and to pay property and income tax and only £3% allowed to us for our money'.

The governors refused his application for the reinvestment of 'his' money, pointing out they were its trustees. However, surprisingly, but perhaps due to Morgan's persistence and importunity, Marshall's Trustees now came to the rescue and offered a grant of £200 which was met by a Bounty grant of half its value, thus making (with Thirlwall's benefaction) £600 in all. Half of this, £300, was spent on the work of building outhouses and walling the grounds during 1862-3.[6]

Bishop Thirlwall, shown this correspondence by the Bounty governors, replied in his terse style on 3 June 1862:

The letter of which you have sent me a copy is very characteristic of the writer. Mr Morgan is not generally deficient in intelligence, but where his own interests are concerned I have found it beyond his power to listen to reason.

Thirlwall had told him that instead of grumbling at the smallness of the grant for the Bounty fund 'he ought to consider himself extremely fortunate. But I believe that it would be impossible to induce him to take that view of the subject'. However, the bishop added that he would have been happier if the governors had made a larger grant, so increasing the very small income of that populous parish, for 'the parsonage having been build on too large a scale to meet the requirements of the Ecclesiastical Commissioners, is, as Mr Morgan, I believe truly represents, rather a burden than a benefit'. Thirlwall thus considered the Llansamlet case worthy of a larger benefaction and urged the governors to reconsider their position. But the grant was not increased, though another benefaction was augmented as we have noted.

****

Morgan was also perpetual curate of St John's juxta Swansea, a parish so small it was not considered worthy of an entry in the 1842 *Clergy List*. This parish had been held from time immemorial with Llangyfelach. The vicar of that parish had held a Welsh service in the church on Sunday afternoons but '[n]othing more was regularly done' wrote E. G. Williams many years later in his pamphlet about church extension in Swansea,[7] 'except that the people themselves held prayer meetings on weekday evenings'. During the vacancy in Llangyfelach in 1842 the living was attached instead to Llansamlet. Rice Morgan continued the Sunday service with the addition of a weekday evening service, and appointed a curate to serve the parish for him, who was supported by a grant from the Assistant Curates' Society.[8]

At the same time as Morgan was endeavouring to persuade the governors of the Bounty to assist him in the work of building his vicarage wall and outbuildings, he was also in correspondence with the commissioners. He was asking them not only to assist him in this work, but also to bring up the income of the parish of Llansamlet to £150 per annum. After all, he claimed, they were under some obligation to him, as they had forced him to build a house costing £1,300, £700 more than was really required, and which necessitated him finding £150 out of his own pocket for its completion. He begged them, therefore, to have pity upon his poor parish, as well as his successor, who would have to live on the fruits of this one living only. They might care to offer him a grant in return for the benefaction he had received from Marshall's Charity, he suggested, as the Bounty governors had already done. But such a 'double grant', the commissioners replied, was against the rules of both organisations and consequently they could not offer him a grant to meet a benefaction which had already been met with a grant by another body. This infuriated Morgan. Writing in hard fury he informed the commissioners that it had been their 'disposition' right from the beginning 'to throw me overboard and overlook my case by hook or by crook'. It was not sufficient to say that because one body had given a grant the other could not do so. They had powers to alter their regulations: 'where there is a will, there is a way.' The governors reply was brief and to the point for they were used to dealing with disappointed and difficult clergymen. As the £200 benefaction was now the property of the living it could not be used as another benefaction.

Similar letters arrived at the commissioners' office from Morgan during May and July of 1863. His living worth £130 had to support his wife, four children and a fine house. In December Morgan heard that the living of Llangyfelach had been granted an augmentation of £142 to increase its stipend to £300 on the grounds of its population. It had a population of over 10,000 people. Morgan wrote in some fury that his population was 5,603 but he was forced to work the parish in two divisions, one around the parish church and the other consisting of Kilvey and Foxhole, where he had a church, two schoolrooms and two curates paid for by the proprietors of the copperworks. To all intents and purposes this was a separate district, although it had not been legally constituted. But he thought that its population had been returned in the census with that of Swansea, rather than with his own parish. Morgan obviously believed that if he could produce evidence that his parish had a greater population than the 5,603 declared in the last census he would obtain a similar increase in his stipend as had the vicar of Llangyfelach.

Tracings of the boundaries were produced at the request of the commissioners. The letter which accompanied them contained a tirade against those absentee landlords who got rich from the mineral wealth under the land, but left the poor vicar without his tithes. What made the matter worse, he now claimed, was that the greater tithes belonged to the see of St David's, and the lease had been renewed three times since 1840, the date of Bishop Thirlwall's appointment. When the lease expired an income of £200 would revert to the commissioners. The lessee was a Mrs Perret of Cheltenham who had no connection with the parish. The only favourable thing which Morgan could write about her was that she was between 84 and 85 years of age, and so the lease would soon lapse. The letter concluded with an apology. He had been mistaken about the population. It was only 5,000 or thereabouts: Kilvey's figures had been included in Llansamlet's. But obviously Morgan believed that if he lost one argument it was worth starting another, namely for an augmentation of his stipend on the grounds of a local claim against the commissioners.

The commissioners did not take offence. Morgan must have been deeply surprised to read that they intended to augment all livings in public patronage, as was his own, where the population was recorded as over 4,000 in the last census. What Morgan did not know, and presumably the commissioners did, was that there was a sting in the tail. His abuse of them was going to get a just return.

Morgan was delighted. His letter of application mentioned that he was 'much under the water' with a debt to the sum of

£200 to £300. He had to support and educate his children and there had been a long illness in his family. A local commission was appointed. The first paper of queries was filled in by Morgan himself who then sent it to Edward Squire, the rural-dean and vicar of Swansea, for his signature as Squire had been nominated chairman of the panel. Regarding Morgan's procedure as entirely improper (for the commissioners were meant to investigate the circumstances of the parish, not to countersign the incumbent's own entry), Squire sent it to the bishop. Thirlwall wrote to the commissioners on 20 March 1866:

> I believe however that, without any great stretch of charity, his conduct may be attributed to utter want of judgment and incapacity for business, rather than to a dishonest purpose.

The local commission, reconvened, reported that the population in 1861 was 5,103, the income of the parish £160 gross and £138 net per annum (tithe-rent charge £46, Ecclesiastical Commission £39, Queen Anne's Bounty £53, fees £22, less deductions), but as vicar of St John's Morgan also received an income of £106 net. Morgan however had reported his income as £122 and £90 net respectively. He had underestimated both the tithe income and the fees.

Morgan later apologised for this turn of events. He felt that he alone knew the circumstances of the living, and so he had sent the form to Squire together with a letter requesting that if he doubted the truth of any of his statements he should send for him and meet him. Squire's action had brought 'the Bishop about my ears with a vengeance. I had a regular scolding, probably not without deserving it for my inattention to business and for being such a simpleton'. The discrepancy in fees was because the commissioners had given the average figure over a number of years, while he had returned the figures for the previous year, which was lower than the average as the old graveyard had been shut up by government order some time before, and he was thus deprived of the fees it brought him.

It was at this time that Morgan applied for his perpetual curacy to be declared a vicarage and for his own status to be regulated. As a duly instituted incumbent he would possess the freehold, and no bishop would be able to turn him out without complicated legal procedures. Perhaps after the above episode with Thirlwall Morgan may have wondered about his security of tenure under an episcopal licence. His thankfulness, as well as possibly his relief, was obvious from his letter of 9 April 1866 to Mr Hodgson, the secretary of the Bounty, who appears to have been very sympathetic to Morgan's position:

Many thanks for your kind communication of the 5th instant giving me the Information that the Commissioners have been pleased to pass an Instrument, declaring this Benefice a Vicarage. My wife and children are delighted with it, and they wish me a long life to enjoy it. I feel conscious that I owe this kindness to yourself, and I now most sincerely thank you for it. When I had the pleasure of an interview with you last year at your Office I found at once that you sympathise deeply with the hardworking poor Clergy, and that you wished to encourage us in every possible way. I assure you, I have worked hard and incessantly in this Parish for the last 23 years with very little encouragement, but it appears at last that the time is come for some material assistance, consolation and encouragement. I could never live here with a large family had it not been that I held another small Incumbency with it, and in order to educate six fine children I am obliged to perform 3 full services and preach 3 times every Sunday, besides other incessant Surplice duties . . .

The commissioners also responded favourably to his request for an augmentation on the grounds of population, having accepted the figures given by the local commissioners chaired by Squire. They offered him £162, thus bringing his income up to a round £300 per annum. But there was a condition. This augmentation would only be available when he held his living in conformity with the laws relating to plurality as applicable to new incumbents.

It may well be imagined that Mr Morgan's protests were loud and bitter. At first he appears to have misunderstood the position, and assumed that the commissioners were accusing him of holding two livings illegally. He had held both, he pointed out, since 1842 under a dispensation from the archbishop of Canterbury. The commissioners replied that they had no doubt as to the legality of *his* holding these two benefices. But under the existing laws no new incumbent could do so, and we know that Morgan knew this as well from some of his previous statements. As a condition of receiving his grant Morgan was required to conform to the present laws as though he was a new incumbent, and this meant he had to resign one of his two livings. While the diocesan registrar, Valentine Davies, wrote in his favour, accepting the matter as one of misunderstanding, and stating that this legislation was prospective rather than retrospective, Bishop Thirlwall was less obliging. Morgan had failed to give the commission adequate assistance by not keeping any account of his fee income. The separation of his two benefices was greatly desired for his incumbency at St John's operated as a bar to church extension in Swansea and had prevented some 'most important aid' from being received from an influential layman. This, we know from other sources, was John Henry Vivian of Singleton, the proprietor of the Hafod Copper Works and the principal employer in St John's parish. He had established schools in the parish and had promised to provide a church and supplement the income of its incumbent from his own resources. But the bishop refused to institute an incumbent until the parish became vacant, and Vivian refused to build a church for a pluralist. Instead his firm paid for a curate who conducted services for the Hafod area in one of the school buildings. But it was later said that the Church had little impact in that community because the people were resentful that they did not have an incumbent of their own and a parish church in their own locality.[9]

Morgan had by now taken expert advice, and he wrote in reply to the commissioners on 14 June 1866 querying their assertions. According to the acts quoted by them, 1 & 2 Victoria c. 106 and 13 & 14 Victoria c. 93, an exemption was given to those pluralities which were within three miles of one another by the nearest road, and the annual value of one of the livings did not exceed £100. He believed that both these requirements applied to his plurality, and understood that these matters had been inquired into when he had obtained a dispensation from the archbishop in 1842. Even if it proved to be the case that the distance was more than three miles, he believed that the peculiar case of St John's Church needed to be taken into account and allowed in his favour. The church in fact was situated in the parish of Swansea and was more than half a mile away from its own parish boundary. If it had been built within the actual parish it would only have been two miles from Llansamlet Church.

As he was laying plans to build a new church for St John's parish within its existing boundaries, Morgan wrote that he felt loath to give up the parish until he had completed this good work. However the heaviest consideration in his mind was the thought of parting with a congregation he loved 'most dearly' – 'I have been the means, under the blessing of God, of uniting together about 350 communicants'. There was also another local precedent. Llangyfelach had been augmented two years earlier but its vicar had not been required to give up his incumbency of Morriston. Indeed, the commissioners had even given him a grant of £50 for a curate. This vicar had only two children to support. He had six. Why should this vicar be dealt with more leniently than he, who presumably could claim in his favour an over-production of infants? As an afterthought Morgan remembered his other church at Kilvey. This was only one mile from St John's Church. He therefore prayed the commissioners to reconsider their decision though if he had to submit to it he would be humble enough to do so.

The commissioners repeated their original proposal, and Morgan now resorted to the ploy of confusion. Could they put their statements in plain language rather than in legal words? He now claimed that his patron was not willing for him to resign the living of St John's and had told him that if he continued in the parish he would build a new church and provide a curate to serve it. In the light of Thirlwall's previous remarks these statements appear to be rather dubious. The commissioners now told him in very plain language that he should either resign one benefice or the other. Morgan, exasperated, wrote in reply on 23 November 1866: 'I am not such a noodle to suffer myself to be deprived of my just and legal rights according to the laws of my country, without struggling against it.' Why should he be treated differently from his next door neighbour? If the commissioners insisted on this matter, he would 'ventilate' it before public opinion.

It was not until December of that year that Morgan realised he needed to prove his various assertions. He obtained a surveyor who certified that the distance between the two churches was under three miles. He also provided a statement of the annual income of St John's Church, indicating a parliamentary grant of £20, the rental of land in the parishes of Bishopston at £21 and Llangennith at £24, two cottages at Kenfig let at £26, and surplice fees of £6. All this, less taxes and rates, came to £95 net. These statements were duly sent up to London along with his offer to meet the commissioners' secretary at his London office, for he was fetching his 'little boy' for the holidays from St John's Foundation School at Hampton. While Morgan was informed that he could not be seen on this occasion, it is clear that considerable attention was paid to his arguments and their accompanying statements. It was now agreed that the two churches were within the distance allowed for pluralities, and the income of one was also under the value of £100. His grant of £162 was now allowed and his income from Llansamlet increased to £300 per annum. But though he was successful Morgan wrote on 14 June 1867 that he felt 'doomed' and heart sickened at all the trouble he had been subjected to by this affair. And he had been proved right in the end too!

But the battle now continued on another front.

For the previous five or six years, Morgan wrote in September 1868, he had been taking three full services each Sunday. He was now in ill-health and his doctor insisted he did less work. For 30 years he had worked almost single-handed in his parish (a rather far-fetched statement), and almost as a reward for such diligence he requested a grant from the commissioners for the services of an assistant curate. He based his application on the understanding that on the leaseholder's death the great tithes of the parish would fall into the commissioners' hands, and thus enable him to request assistance under a local claim. These were worth £200 per annum, and from this sum he suggested a sum of £40 for a deacon or £60 for a priest. His application was declined because he held the parish in plurality.

Five years later E. Lloyd Hughes wrote to the commissioners from the Vicarage, Llansamlet. It was 7 June 1873, and Hughes was applying for a curate's grant. The bishop had appointed him curate in charge as the vicar was now in a state of imbecility and his doctors considered that his was a hopeless case. For the previous five years the parish had been neglected because of his illness. The vicar had given an English service in the morning at the parish church and a Welsh service in the evening, with the result that both sides felt neglected with only one service and instead frequented the Nonconformist chapels. The services of a curate were desperately required in order to remedy this position.

The commissioners noted their earlier statement and repeated it. While the parish was held in plurality they were unable to assist it.

Hughes, however, had Morgan's fire in him, and refused to accept this answer. He was sorry, he wrote, to hear of this technical objection. The present condition of the Church in Wales ought to overrule all such technicalities. The vicar's position was theoretical. He was a hopeless imbecile. His relatives had wanted him to resign but because he had been certified as insane no such resignation could take effect. This decision of the commissioners was playing into the hands of the Nonconformists, who were seeking to disestablish the Church. Thankfully the commissioners reconsidered the case and allowed the grant.

Morgan died on 7 March 1874. His death allowed the two parishes to be separated. Thomas Walters became his successor at Llansamlet and reorganised the parish and rebuilt the parish church. Messrs Vivians and Sons, the patrons of the living of St John's, re-endowed the living and had it transferred to Hafod, giving it a new parish church plus a stipend for the incumbent. The old parish church became St Matthew's Church, served by the clergy of St Mary's as the Welsh church for the parish of Swansea. The daughter church at Kilvey became a separate parish in 1886.

****

Morgan Rice Morgan was a pluralist of the old regime. While he was a noted evangelical preacher within the Welsh speaking community of Wales,[10] and a conscientious parish priest, he was true to his west Walian principles in looking after his own interests as well – a trend much noted by his diocesan bishop. His endeavours to serve his parish were hampered, rather than assisted, by the Ecclesiastical Commission. True, they provided him with a more substantial stipend, but what they gave they had taken away by requiring him to build a gentleman's residence as a vicarage, which had become a burden rather than a benefit to him. Furthermore, the poverty of his earlier days had driven him to find alternative employment as incumbent of a neighbouring parish. Tragically, there was little provision made for clergymen to retire at that time, and thus the good work he had managed to do in gathering together three congregations had been lost by the end of his life, when old age and mental illness had taken their toll. Ironically, today, any cleric who would take on a neighbouring parish besides his own would be received with open arms by most bishops, who would also provide him with a modest house undistinguishable from its neighbours.

ENDNOTES

The main source used for this chapter has been the papers of the Ecclesiastical Commission and of Queen Anne's Bounty which are in the custody of the Representative Body of the Church in Wales.

1   T W Barker, *Diocese of St Davids: Particulars relating to the Endowment of Livings* (Carmarthen, 1907), I 186f.
2   E G Williams, *Move On* (Swansea, 1889) p. 12; Stephen Hughes, *Copperopolis* (Aberystwyth, 2000), p. 259.
3   *Reports of the Commissioners of Inquiry into the State of Education in Wales* (London, 1848), pp. 121f.
4   *Report*, pp. 120f.
5   J Ginswick (ed), *Labour and the Poor in England and Wales 1849-51* (London, 1983), p. 185.
6   Barker, *St Davids*, p. 187.
7   Williams, *Move On*, pp. 9f.
8   *Ecclesiastical Gazette*, 1843, pp. 46f.
9   Williams, *Move On*, p. 10.
10 For an account of Morgan's preaching in Welsh, "his rare oratorical powers . . . like a strong angel flying in the midst of heaven", see *Cardiff and Merthyr Guardian*, 7 September 1850, p. 3. He also hosted clerical (or preaching) meetings at Llansamlet. These were much frequented by the evangelical clergy at the time (ibid, 7 June 1862, p. 6). He preached, for example, the Welsh sermon at the opening of Michaelston Parish Church, near Port Talbot, in May 1851: Granville James, *A Brief History of the Parish of Llanfihangel Ynys Afan* (1999), pp. 54f.

Richard Williams Morgan:
Patriarch, Priest and Romantic

Tregynon in the mid-nineteenth century was an isolated village, dominated by the big house of Gregynog. Almost hidden in the hills of east Montgomeryshire, its ethos was a frontier one where suspicions lingered and reserve was the operative mode. Writing nearly a hundred years later about the neighbouring parish of Manafon R. S. Thomas noted the prevailing tension of these small communities where the traditions and feuds of the past were often more important than present or future concerns.[1]

It was to this small parish of Tregynon that Richard Williams Morgan was appointed perpetual curate in 1843. His sense of discontent about his circumstances in his parish may be seen in the two following extracts taken from his book, *The Verities of the Church*, published in 1849:

How is it that, amongst the many who present themselves to the nation, part as the friends, part as the reformers of the Church, not one has stood forth to advocate the claims of that ill-paid, ill-used, but laborious section of the clergy, perpetual curates under lay rectors? Ecclesiastical rectors are obliged to pay their curates in a certain proportion to the value of the living: what reason can be assigned why lay rectors should not be obliged to do the same?

The circumstances in which the present publication originated are shared by the author with many of his brother clergy in the Church. Placed in the pastoral care of an

Tregynon Parish Church in the 1870s.

isolated rural parish, with but little society at command, he found himself obliged to fall back for mental occupation on his own resources . . .[2]

During his time at Tregynon Morgan wrote a considerable number of books and pamphlets. If they reveal his concern for an old fashioned high church theology, a romantic view of history, and an emerging Welsh nationalism, they also reveal a mind which, fasting in a wilderness of discontent and in an agony of loneliness (for he was unmarried), seems to have become somewhat unhinged.

Richard Williams Morgan started life well. Born in 1812, his father was vicar of Llanfor near Bala, and his mother's father was John Williams, *Yr Hen Syr*, headmaster of the celebrated grammar school at Ystrad Meurig in Cardiganshire, which was licensed by the bishops of St David's for training men for holy orders. A number of these bishops, it is said, alleged that no candidates presented for ordination compared with Williams's pupils in classical and theological knowledge. Under him the school achieved a recognition throughout Wales. Morgan's uncles on his mother's side included David Williams, a fellow of Wadham College who succeeded his father as headmaster of the school, and John Williams, archdeacon of Cardigan, called by Sir Walter Scott, a close friend, the first schoolmaster in Europe during his principalship of the Edinburgh Academy. An uncle by marriage was Sir David Davies, a royal physician to both King William IV and Queen Victoria.[3] With such a wealth of family behind him, including an internationally known schoolteacher and archdeacon (with whom he seems to have been on rather close terms), and a royal doctor, Morgan must have believed that good fortune should have come his way. It did not. And in its failure bitterness and resentment appears to have taken its place.

Educated by his uncle at Edinburgh, where he received a solid classical and theological training, Morgan should have been destined for one of the ancient universities. But here was the first default, for his lot was cast at St David's College, Lampeter, which he entered at the age of 28 in March 1840.[4] It was in the normal course of events a late age at which to start such training, and one wonders if Morgan had been articled beforehand to a solicitor, or had acted as a schoolmaster himself. Ordained in October 1841 by the bishop of St Asaph, his title was to the curacy of Mochdre, then in the diocese of St David's, to which was soon added the perpetual curacy of Tregynon in the diocese of St Asaph. Presented by Lord Sudeley, the lay impropriator, Morgan had undertaken the duties of this parish for some months previously for the preceding incumbent. That was the highest dignity he ever achieved within the Church. St Asaph was his father's diocese, but might not his uncle have found something better for him in the diocese of St David's than Mochdre? Apparently not, for by then his uncle was not in good repute, or at least not in those circles which Morgan would have described as the Anglo-Welsh ecclesiastical hierarchy.

According to the returns presented to the 1851 religious census Tregynon had a population of 718, accommodation within the church for 260 of these people, and an average congregation of between 90 and 150, with 129 present at the afternoon service on the day of the census. There was only one service each Sunday, alternating between morning and afternoon, for Morgan, as already noted, served as curate to an absentee incumbent at Mochdre. There he had a morning service with 50 worshippers on that census day. He received £50 for this curacy, and returned his income at Tregynon as £83, consisting of land worth £60 per annum, a permanent endowment of £20, and the remainder in fees.[5] Writing in 1853 he pointed out that the distance between these two churches was 10 miles, with 'roads of the roughest and most exposed description, presenting scarcely a mile of level or trotting ground in their whole extent'. During the previous eleven years he reckoned he had ridden between twenty and thirty thousand miles on this route alone, and during one period of eight Sundays had had to ride through storms and floods so that he was unable to officiate even once in dry clothes. His home was a cottage (Claremont Cottage) allowed him rent free by Lord Sudeley, as there was no parsonage, and his stipend from Mochdre barely covered the expenses of a horse and groom. On the £70 net value of Tregynon he maintained a household of a housekeeper and a female servant, besides this groom.[6]

It is hardly surprising that Morgan should have endeavoured to increase his income from Tregynon. We have already noted his indirect protest about the impropriator of the parish, his patron Lord Sudeley, who took the tithes and allowed him only the ancient stipend of £20, probably awarded in the Tudor period, which had never been increased to take into account inflation. In correspondence with the Ecclesiastical Commission, which was regulating the episcopal and capitular incomes of the Church and applying the residue to the needs of 'populous districts', Morgan wrote that his parishioners, with but one exception, were small tenant farmers and labourers, who were in constant 'need of Christian charity and assistance'. On his small income he could hardly afford to offer them either. But the commissioners replied that a parish like his was outside the terms of their remit, particularly as it was in private patronage. Morgan also applied to Queen Anne's Bounty, an organisation devoted to caring for the needs of small parishes, but all it could offer him was a grant against a benefaction of £200, but this, as Morgan replied, was quite outside his power to secure. By 1852 the correspondence had become acrimonious with the commissioners, as Morgan continually repeated his requests, stating that as far as he understood the funds at their disposal were in order to 'redress . . . that most crying necessity, the augmentation of such impoverished and impoverishing livings as Tregynon'. He was equally angered by the refusal of Lord Sudeley as the lay impropriator to assist the parish financially for this refusal meant that 'the working curate should be made to suffer . . . after eleven years severe and patient toil in the Church'. By the time that Morgan resigned the parish its buildings and glebe land were out of repair, and it was impossible to recover from him the dilapidations required to put them in order as he had been declared effectually bankrupt. As a result Lord Sudeley found it hard to obtain a successor, and consequently offered his share of the tithes as a benefaction to the commissioners. It was too late to benefit Morgan, but one has the distinct impression that his lordship was not really prepared to help the parish while Morgan remained as its incumbent because of his unstable and ill-disciplined character.[7]

****

During these years of his active residence, 1842-53, Morgan wrote a large number of books. The majority of them attracted considerable attention, and indicate a well-read man with a scholarly mind, but a somewhat disorganised methodology, combined with an naiveté and an ability to take far too much on trust. But the latter was equally the fault of many distinguished scholars of his own generation.

His major theological work, *Notes on Various Distinctive Verities of the Christian Church*, published in 1849, is a maze of random reflections on over two hundred subjects, and was the subject of an article by Owain W. Jones in *Province*. Although he mentioned the *Tracts for the Times* and was clearly influenced by them, a great deal of Morgan's theological background may have come from his acquaintanceship with the Episcopal Church of Scotland, which retained a high church, almost non-juror-type theology. This was the theology of Laud and the seventeenth century English theologians, so that Morgan could write in his preface to this book that he had a 'deep founded affection for the Catholic faith, as guarded and propagated by the Apostolic Church of England'. He thus emphasised that the apostolic succession was required for a valid celebration of the Eucharist; proclaimed baptismal regeneration; the erastian union between Church and State, if not denied, was at least declared inessential; more reverence needed to be given to the patristic tradition rather than to the sixteenth century reformers (through he regarded the liturgy those reformers wrote as showing 'the beauty of Christianity'), and strangely, but characteristically, he asserted that the Church of England united in her priesthood the triple succession of the ancient British, ancient Irish and ancient Roman churches. The reviews were not unfavourable. Rowland Williams, vice-principal of St David's College, Lampeter, commented that for literary power and 'apparent earnestness of thought' the book would do honour to the pupil of any college, though it were possible that time and reflection 'may teach its able writer to modify some of his stronger sayings'. Such words were ominous, although in the context of the book they possibly referred to Morgan's deep seated dislike of 'papistry' and his equal hatred of 'Geneva', and such comments as the one about the State's refusal to place on the archiepiscopal throne of Canterbury a man equal to its responsibilities.[8]

One of these themes, and another we will note later, emerge in what was probably his earliest publication. This was a pamphlet, *Maynooth and St Asaph: or, the Religious Policy of the Conservative Cabinet Considered*, published in 1845. His criticism of Sir Robert Peel shows all the marks of a disillusioned follower. Although this may have been because of Peel's religious policy, there may also have been a personal element in it, as Morgan's uncle, Archdeacon Williams, believed he had lost the see of St Davids in 1840, in spite of repeated promises, because the administration of the day was Whig and not Tory.

Morgan thus wrote:

> He [Peel] favours schism and dissent in England, and
> Papistry in Ireland: he gives his right hand to an
> heterogeneous hydra that bears a different religious creed on
> every head, agreeing only in the singular crotchet that no
> nation has the right to establish and support Christianity –
> and his left he resigns to a foreign church, the head of which
> is at Rome, though its arms are everywhere, and which in
> return for his amazing cordiality presents him with her little
> finger.

In Ireland Peel's financial assistance to an anti-Protestant
college was the prelude to his endowing the whole Roman
Church in that country, argued Morgan, while in England [sic]
he was destroying an Anglican bishopric. (This was a reference
to the Ecclesiastical Commissioners' desire to unite the two sees
of Bangor and St Asaph in order to form a new see at
Manchester). But the Roman Irish had stabbed England in the
back all too often, and were 'everlasting beggars, soaking upon
hard-worked, hard-taxed, hard-struggling neighbours'. In order
to pacify the inhabitants of Ireland in this way the true
Protestant Church was discounted and its work of Biblical
witness 'starved' and 'disowned'. Instead the Roman priests in
Ireland had been allowed to turn 'their chapels into agitation
theatres, delivering fanatic diatribes against the Saxon, and
working up their audience to riot', and encouraging
disobedience against all those in authority. It was not feasible,
therefore, to place the pacification of Ireland on the shoulders
on the Irish priests especially when that policy offered nothing
in return, not even a solemn vow that in exchange for this vast
measure the Roman Church would encourage its members to be
good citizens of the United Kingdom, and not agitate and
conspire to obtain the repeal of the union.[9]

Another pamphlet further expressed Morgan's fear of

Roman Catholicism. This was his *A Vindication of the Church of England in Reply to Viscount Fielding, on his Recent Secession to the Church of Rome* of 1851. Lord Fielding, a prominent landowner in the diocese of St Asaph, had not only become a Roman convert together with his wife, but had given the church he was building at Pantasaph to that allegiance as well. His conversion, wrote Morgan, had 'struck like an electric pang through the whole body of the Church in North Wales'. Although he accepted the right of private judgment, and that Lord Fielding had as much right to his opinions as he had to his, Morgan wanted to prove to him that in quitting the Church of England for Rome, he had 'left . . . a more pure for a less pure Church'. Thus Morgan attempted to establish that Rome's claim to universal sovereignty over the Church of Christ because of its alleged Petrine foundation and succession was a false claim. Rather she had mixed the 'pure Word of God' with semi-human, semi-divine apocryphal books; had endeavoured to solve 'a high and spiritual mystery by the gross physical tenet of "Transubstantiation"', and in her mariolatry had made "a similitude of the Lord Jesus Christ", "our God and Saviour"; of a *female*, "the Blessed Virgin".' Morgan also denied that his own Church was a protestant one, as Fielding had maintained. Rather she was 'The Reformed Apostolic Catholic Church of England'. Undoubtedly, part of the background of this polemic was the introduction of the Roman hierarchy into England and Wales in 1850, which had aroused considerable hostility to the Roman Catholic Church within the nation at large.[10]

All this may suggest to our minds that Morgan was a loyal son of the Anglican Church, but even here we may suggest there was a tinge of romanticism. And this romanticism, this speculative romanticism, comes out strongly in his historical and literary work. But then the age in which he lived shared this interest, witness Tennyson with his chivalrous knights and the paintings of the pre-Raphaelites. Thus in many of his pseudo-historical works Morgan endeavoured to prove and even add to Celtic mythology. His book, *The British Kymru or Britons of Cambria*, claimed to establish the genealogy of the royal line of Britain from Gomer and Brutus, commencing with Noah and ending with Victoria via Constantine the Great and Howel Dda. Significantly it was translated into Welsh by another pseudo-historian, John Williams ab Ithel. Another similar title, possibly an update of part of the above, *A History of Britain from the Flood to AD 700*, was published in 1857. The British, that is the Welsh, were now traced from the lost ten tribes of Israel, while a great deal of unscholarly reliance was placed on Geoffrey of Monmouth's more bizarre accounts in his history. The theme of St Paul having visited Britain, noted here, was more fully expanded in *St Paul in Britain*. In this book Morgan developed the thesis that the Celtic countries were ideal for the reception of Christianity as the Druidic religion ran almost parallel to it, particularly with its beliefs in the immortality of the soul and vicarious atonement. Consequently Celtic religion came directly from Jerusalem rather than from Rome, and as such it was pure and undefiled. This, of course, was in part a restatement of the Celtic myth so beloved of the Welsh sixteenth-century reformers, and which was endorsed by a considerable number of scholars thereafter, including Bishops Stillingfleet of Worcester and Burgess of St David's. This particular book, dedicated to Connop Thirlwall, bishop of St David's, in recognition of 'his conscientious mastery, as a bishop of souls, of the language of his people', was republished in an edited version as late as the 1950s by the British Israelite movement.[11]

'Reposing one wintry evening in my cottage at Tregynon, with Aristotle's Treatise on the Drama in my hand, I abandoned myself to reveries connected with the Era of that magnificent philosopher,' wrote Morgan as an introduction to his poem, *Ida de Gallis, a Tragedy of Powis Castle*, published in 1851. As a result Morgan determined to write a classical tragedy relating to his own native land of 'Venadotia', and which would embrace the 'mystic land of Avallon'. His initial wish, wrote a reviewer, to use the ancient Greek drama to bring to the minds of the people the far greater truths of the Catholic faith, rather than the heathen religion they had previously held, was only feebly set forth in the mouth of one of the characters. The same reviewer argued that while many parts of the poem were striking and at times eloquent, Morgan carried a little too far his concept of 'the simplicity of expression'. Another work was *Raymond de Monthault, the Lord Marcher*, which related to a legend of medieval Wales. These works are now long forgotten, and one wonders to what extent they were purchased in his own day; possibly Morgan spent a little too much of his meagre financial resources on vanity publishing.[12]

With this background of romance and historical fiction, it is hardly to be wondered at that Morgan was involved in the eisteddfod movement, both at local and provincial level. He was one of those who endeavoured to re-establish the Powys provincial eisteddfod during the 1850s, but his involvement in the Llangollen eisteddfod of 1858 under the bardic name of Môr Morion was more infamous. At that time the movement was ill-organised and every local group did its own thing. Morgan, with John Williams Ab Ithel and Joseph Hughes, all clerics, were the main organisers of this eisteddfod and, it seems, the beneficiaries of its substantial profits. They appeared in the most extreme of druidical costumes; too many of the prizes were awarded to Ab Ithel's family, and the one major work which appeared for competition, Thomas Stephens' *Madoc*, was denied a prize because it suggested that the legend of Madoc's discovery of America might not be true. All this made this eisteddfod the laughing stock of Wales, with the result that others, more concerned with the reputation of the eisteddfod movement, determined to organise the events more properly, and so commenced its modern-day mystique.[13]

****

Quite clearly, Morgan inherited his archidiaconal uncle's bias against the Anglo-Welsh hierarchy of Wales, or indeed of the Anglo-Welsh establishment in general. Resentment was coupled with reason in his uncle's assault on this hierarchy, and he genuinely believed he could redress some of the wrongs of the diocese of St David's and the Welsh Church in general had he become its bishop. His nephew went further, and not only allowed the bitterness to predominate but became almost paranoid in his attack on his own bishop, Thomas Vowler Short, of St Asaph. The archdeacon, in his aptly worded title *On the Inexpediency, Folly and Sin of a 'Barbarian Episcopate' in a Christian Principality* (1858), had claimed that the appointment of non Welsh-speaking bishops in Wales was part of a Hanoverian plot to subdue the Principality. The native clergy were denied the prizes of the Church, becoming (as others put it) the hewers of wood and the drawers of water. Instead the prizes went to the relations and friends of the English bishops, who, of course, spoke no Welsh themselves. Williams wrote about the requirements the Anglo-Welsh bishops ought to have considered before they accepted their sees from an English government. He pointed out, for example, that the Book of Common Prayer and the Welsh Bible never conceived of there being a non-Welsh bishop in a Welsh see (the consecration of a bishop in the Welsh book allowed another bishop to act for the archbishop if he, the archbishop, did not speak Welsh); the 34th article concerned speaking in an unknown tongue, while in the consecration service the new bishop was asked if he was persuaded that he was called to this office. These restraints, he argued, should have been well-known to the then bishops in Wales because of a clause which had failed in an 1836 parliamentary bill, which required the Welsh bishops, as well as their clergy, to speak the language of the people. And even though Lord John Russell had declared that he would act in the spirit of that clause in any future appointment, he broke that promise by appointing Vowler Short to the see of St Asaph.

Short, who as bishop of Sodor and Man had been acting for the previous bishop, Carey, was clearly aware of the bilingual nature of the diocese and of his own inability to speak Welsh, but was prepared to accept the nomination. It was Short's friendship with the world – his love of better things, that made him accept this appointment, alleged Williams. As a result the bishop would face the enmity of God, for he knew the position of his diocese, he was aware that the growth of dissent throughout the Principality was due to the Anglo-Welsh bishops, and he must have realised that only bishops and clergy able to preach in the Welsh language could win back the Welsh-speaking people to the Church. Thus, Williams concluded, Short went 'forth to his diocese, and for ten years has practically proved by his continuous lingual incapacity that the Holy Ghost had not called him, otherwise he would have granted him the necessary gifts without which he cannot discharge the ordinary duties of his office'. The depth of Williams's bitterness, which was national as well as personal, emerges in an address to these Anglo-Welsh bishops:

You are, and have been nothing, mere nullities, vain occupiers of spiritual seats, without the power of conferring any spiritual benefit on the poor people committed to your care. But, in another sense, you have *not* been nullities. Your example, in publicly trampling under foot all the obligations you were under to confess the truth and to enforce, at least by your own practice, the holy reverence due to solemn oaths and Christian charity, has served, no doubt, if not as a stimulant, yet certainly not as an obstructor, to that flood of wickedness, profligacy, and disgusting immorality by which Wales is said to have been overwhelmed . . .

It was hardly surprising, therefore that the Welsh people believed that the prelates had been appointed to act as propagators of the English language in Wales. Before the

Anglo-Welsh prelates came into Wales there was no Nonconformity, but now, because of their neglect, Wales had become a nation of Nonconformists.[14]

Such were the views of Archdeacon Williams, and however much his words expressed his disappointment at not obtaining the Welsh mitre he craved for, there were many who still believed he spoke the truth. It hardly mattered that a defence could be made for such prelates, or that they were no better and no worse than their English counterparts, or even that the origins of dissent were far more complicated than the simple formula set out above; the seeds of resentment and bitterness on the part of the native Welsh clergy meant that this is what they wished to believe. And their most eloquent voice during the mid-nineteenth century was that of Richard Williams Morgan.

His three pamphlets on the subject, *Amddiffiniad yr Iaith Gymraeg* ['A Defence of the Welsh Language'], *The Church and its Episcopal Corruptions in Wales; an Appeal to the People of England* and his *Scheme for the Reconstruction of the Church Episcopate and its Patronage in Wales*, might have achieved far more recognition had his ideas been more temperate. Even his uncle, who quoted a long extract from the second title as an appendix to his own work acknowledged this, perhaps a little apologetically, by stating '[t]he "acrimony" shown in the publication plainly shows that the writer deeply feels that he has been wrongfully persecuted by episcopal tyranny, but no bitterness of spirit can invalidate the facts adduced by him in support of his statement.'[15] The *Ecclesiastic*, in a review of the same pamphlet, though accepting a certain truth in his allegations, and accepting that the Anglo-Welsh system had brought the Welsh Church to the verge of destruction, felt the violent language used and the acrimony expressed in it would injure his case, and that Morgan was seriously at fault in this respect.[16]

Both these works extended and clarified Morgan's arguments in his first pamphlet, *Maynooth and St Asaph*. Here the same classic arguments used by Williams are found: a downtrodden Welsh clergy, an alien episcopate who had introduced their relations and friends into the better livings and so plundered the Church (an argument drawn from A.J. Johnes' extraordinary influential work about the causes of dissent in Wales), and a dissent caused not by doctrinal differences or indifference to religion or even to the Church (for the dissenters crowded into churches to hear good Welsh preaching), but rather by this foreign dominance. It may well be that Morgan was stunned into action, as many of his contemporaries were, by the desire of the Ecclesiastical Commission to rationalise the diocesan and episcopal structure of England and Wales. Instead of increasing the number of what was an unpopular breed, it proposed to amalgamate a number of sees in order to establish new dioceses in the manufacturing districts of England. The proposals roused the diocese of St Asaph (which was to be amalgamated with the diocese of Bangor) and stirred up much thought about the role of a bishop, as well as creating further resentment in Wales about the so-called alien episcopate. One wonders how much Morgan's ecclesiology was shaped by this long, well-organised and eventually successful agitation.

Morgan's first pamphlet, published in Welsh and comprising two long letters which had appeared in the *Carnarvon and Denbigh Herald, Amddiffiniad yr Iaith Gymraeg*, attacked the use of the English language by the Established Church in Wales. The Welsh people's rejection of this Church was God's judgement upon it for its neglect of the Welsh language. He also criticised the Welsh bishops and the Welsh members of parliament for failing to assert Welsh interests in London: the latter, he wrote, were unable to 'raise between them as much spirit as a gosling or a clucking old hen'. Morgan demanded Welsh bishops for the Welsh Church and Welsh judges for the nation, asserting that every public post in Wales, from the bishop to the postman, should be filled by Welsh-speaking people.

Possibly because this pamphlet had a wider circulation in Wales than the others, it achieved the distinction of Ellis Owen Ellis producing a cartoon based upon it. This appeared in a satirical but short-lived Welsh periodical, *Y Punch Cymraeg*. Ellis certainly sympathised with Morgan's cause, and in his cartoon he attacked the bishops as the agents of Anglicisation and of a covert popery. Morgan, holding a leek, is depicted whipping three of the four Welsh bishops (Thirlwall is excluded as he had learnt Welsh) over Offa's Dyke and into a fiery dragon's mouth. A spoof quotation from the Koran provided a caption which noted that the 'Chain of Succession' had broken because 'of too many Puseyites trying to climb up it to the land of glory'.

An editorial further extended the argument, making use of Archdeacon Williams's pamphlet but going far beyond him in vehemence. The editor wrote:

Stick at it, Death! You're serving a nation today. Over Offa's Dyke at a gallop fly the arrogant plunderers who have been shameless enough to take tens of thousands of pounds of the people's money year after year, when they know, yes, they *know* that the Almighty has never fitted them to labour in the Welsh Vineyard. They are foreign to the feelings, the language and the national customs of the Welsh; and mortal enemies to everything with a Welsh quality to it. In fact, the plague of English Bishops in Wales is just one instance of the everlasting enmity of the English to the language and nationality of the Welsh. And how can officers bred like this in treachery, and who keep their thrones through violence, expect the blessing of Heaven on their work? Poor devils, they think that the mere tinkling of the Chain of Succession in the ears of the simple Welsh will bring them rushing back to their Old Mother like a swarm of bees back to the hive. This is their mistake: they treat the Welsh more like irrational animals than men that from the womb, through the Sunday School, know the Holy Scriptural way to salvation.

If Morgan was gratified by such publicity, he was also encouraged to imitate such scurrility.[17]

In his second pamphlet, Morgan resumed his general complaints, but now attacked the government as the agent of these abuses, which had left the Welsh episcopate as Popish as it had ever been in the pre-reformed Church. Its 'State-Bishops' had 'violated, rejected, trampled under foot' every principle of the Reformation. Dr Vowler Short, for example, could not 'in the language of the Church in which he is a Bishop', read a syllable of the Holy Scriptures, baptise an infant, catechise a child, celebrate the rite of confirmation, ascertain the qualifications of his examining chaplains, examine candidates for Holy Orders, preach a word to the people, administer the Holy Eucharist, hold any spiritual conversation with his flock, nor consecrate a church: 'Not a single function of the Episcopate nor of the Priesthood in his own Church can he discharge.' But for this inability Dr Short received an income which would pay the stipends of 40 curates, a life peerage, a palace, and a patronage equivalent to that of four named English bishops. The question was asked, 'Is dishonest, unscrupulous Incompetency thus magnificently rewarded and honoured, corruption or not?' And to make the answer more revealing, Morgan asked questions of Dr Short based on the Scriptures, the Episcopal Consecration Service, the Homilies and Articles of his own Church, all sworn to and consented by him when he became bishop of St Asaph by which time he was well aware that three-fourths of the population of his diocese was Welsh-speaking. A confirmation service is described to illustrate the absurdity of his position. His chaplain had to do the work for him. For another example Morgan referred to the consecration service of a church. When the church at Gorsedd was consecrated to replace the one at Pantasaph lost by the secession of Lord Fielding to Rome, it was commented, 'If Lord Fielding affected Popery he would find it nowhere so rife as the Church he had left.' And when a Welsh curate came to Short to ask him for the vacant living of Gresford, for which he was qualified by language and service as well as the faithful discharge of his duty, he was castigated and scourged by his bishop (who could not discharge one of his duties), for the dreadful sin of worldly-mindedness in a Christian minister. The following week the living was given away to the bishop's brother in law, who spoke no Welsh and had never done a minute's work in the diocese.

Morgan endeavoured to condemn Short by quoting from some of his own publications, and continued: 'The "I", a letter more in favour with Dr Short than all the rest of the Alphabet, expresses the Bishop who cannot discharge one of the duties of his Sacred office towards the people he terms "our People".' All he could offer them, in the words of a title of one of his pamphlets, was 'Hints on vulgar Fractions' for little children. Short, Morgan concluded, was simply an agent of the Whigs who was trying to 'Whiggify the Church' by 'changing every Clergyman into a State-Schoolmaster, and degrading the Church itself, the Ministry of Souls, into a Commercial Academy'. If the people of England did not assist the Welsh to end this state of affairs then the catastrophe of disestablishment would occur, and every acre of the Church's land and every shilling of its tithes would be taken possession of and placed in a more worthy trust for Christian purposes 'by the descendants of those who endowed her for the People and not for a miserable minority.'[18] It was an interesting prophecy to say the least.

The third work, Morgan's scheme for the reconstruction of the Church episcopate, was a more thoroughly nationalistic document, and less abusive than the others. Some of the reforms he advocated were becoming popular movements in his own day, although in many respects he was well in advance of contemporary thinking. Patronage, he argued, should no longer be entrusted to bishops (for too much depended on their whims) save for a few parishes, but rather be determined by seniority of service within a diocese, although he allowed that a parish should be given the power of veto. Too often the good livings were given to mere boys who had never knelt at a Christian's deathbed or converted one sinner from the mistaken folly and error of his ways. This scheme would not only debar such striplings from parishes beyond their ability, but also end the servitude the clergy of the diocese had to give to their bishop because he was the font of most of its patronage. During an episcopal vacancy the beneficed clergy of the diocese should be allowed to submit three names for submission to the Crown, and the Crown would be required to accept one of these names. By this method the bishops would truly be bishops of the people. Morgan also wanted an independent Welsh province, with the archbishopric of St David's restored, writing: 'The English Church has its two Archbishoprics; the Irish Church, its two; even the Scottish Episcopal Church, its Primus. Why should the most ancient of them all be condemned to remain under the effects of a papal Bull, reduced to the suffragan of a See founded centuries after itself?' But even in this pamphlet Morgan could not withhold his criticism of Short. Were his diocese worth but £200 per annum he and Bethell of Bangor would soon demonstrate that they could not 'without forswearing themselves to their consecration vows, attempt to undertake Bishoprics in a Church and over a people of whose language they were utterly ignorant', but as 'Bangor and St Asaph are worth thousands per annum, oaths, sacraments, and Prayer-books go for nothing . . .'[19]

There was one tangible result from all this pamphleteering, although it took some years before its implications could be realised. This was a correspondence between Morgan and W. E. Gladstone, later prime minister, of which Gladstone's reply was subsequently published. It read:

Hawarden, October 4, 1856. Rev. Sir,
You will, I am sure, permit me, in replying to your letter, to waive entering upon those portions of it in which you make

comments as to the character of individuals and against which it would be my duty strongly to protest. In answer to your inquiries as to my intentions with regard to the appointments to the Welsh bishoprics, I must observe that I have no power either as a Privy Councillor or as a Member of Parliament to regulate these appointments; that any attempt made by me to that purpose would probably retard its attainment; and that I would venture to suggest your addressing yourself to those who really possess power over them, or to some of the numerous persons who hold, what I do not hold, that episcopal appointments may properly be used in connection with the objects of political patronage. I deeply lament the estrangement of a people so estimable as the Welsh, from the Church of their country, and I should very gladly see the day when all the occupants of the episcopal sees might be able to communicate with the people in their own language; but I must add, that I think it would be an error to recognise a knowledge of the Welsh language as dispensing with any of the other still more essential qualifications for the episcopal office.[20]

Gladstone thus acted on his own advice when he nominated Joshua Hughes to the bishopric of St Asaph in 1870, and it is tempting to suggest that Morgan may have sown some of the seeds of that appointment in the future premier's mind.

Morgan took an equally direct line by writing on a number of occasions to Lord Derby, the then prime minister, during the vacancy at Bangor in 1859. The closing of the highest offices to Welshmen within the Church 'is the surest method of destroying in every Welsh clergyman all incentive to high exertion or attainments', he wrote, adding that it was unfair to suggest that those Welsh clergymen who wrote in recommending the appointment of a Welsh-speaking man were doing so to further their own individual interests. For himself he had no pretensions to the vacant see, but nevertheless he enclosed a list of his publications to enable Lord Derby to see that there were clergymen of scholarship and literary ability in Wales who were as well qualified as the rest of the Queen's subjects, English or Scotch, for episcopal elevation. But the real necessity was not this, but rather 'a familiar idiomatic acquaintance with the Welsh language, and a hearty fellow-feeling – an identification of the man and his office with the Welsh people'. A national Church needed to be the Church of the producing and working classes, and '[a] preaching Welsh prelate will do more to retrieve the character of the Welsh church with the Welsh people, than a thousand silent volumes in inaccessible libraries'. Only then would the Welsh episcopate be a living force to 'the most ancient, orderly, and least criminal portion of the population of the United Kingdom', instead of 'a dumb, mercenary, repulsive imposition of the state'. It did not matter whether the man appointed was English, Welsh, Scottish or Irish; the necessary qualification was that he had long ministered in the Welsh tongue and within the Welsh Church. Although Morgan wrote that he was convinced that Lord Derby had the true interests of Wales at heart, his next letter revealed that he was rather uncertain about this matter. Rumours had abounded that Maurice Bonnor, vicar of Ruabon and later dean of St Asaph, would be appointed. A further letter of advice followed from Morgan. Bonnor had no real knowledge of Welsh, and had delegated the Welsh duties in his parish to a Welsh curate. Besides this there was an even more fundamental objection. The New Testament indicated that bishops should be the husband of one wife, and Christian tradition had interpreted this to mean that he should not be permitted to re-marry if his wife had died. But Bonnor was 'a Priest of Three Wives' and thus ineligible.

Bonnor was not appointed as bishop, and it is uncertain if he had ever been considered, but the person who was, James Colquhoun Campbell, was the subject of another bitter remonstrance from Morgan. The bishop of Llandaff, Alfred

Ollivant (Morgan's former teacher at Lampeter) and the Marchioness of Bute, Morgan claimed, had brought Campbell's name to the attention of Lord Derby. Ollivant was no judge of a man's linguistic fitness, for he was himself unqualified in any practical way in the Welsh language. Indeed, had Ollivant told the whole truth Campbell would never have been appointed, for he was as unfit as Ollivant for a Welsh see. Besides his church in Merthyr Tydfil was half empty. To appoint a Scotchman to this diocese was equivalent to appointing a Welshman who could speak no English to an English see! However, Morgan soon changed his mind, and although he was politically a Liberal (having changed his opinions over Peel's Irish policy), he now applauded the Tory Lord Derby's appointment. For he had heard that Campbell had ministered in the Welsh tongue to the inhabitants of Merthyr Tydfil, 'the most exhausting, and the least attractive town in the Principality'. Thus, he argued, the prime minister had not only appropriately sought out a bishop from such a parish as Merthyr, but had 'done the Welsh Church the justice for which we agitated the Principality, and we may regard the appointment as the restoration to the Welsh language of the native episcopate'. Furthermore, Lord Derby had shown that the important Welsh parishes in Wales would 'be the nurseries and stepping stones to our Welsh sees', so that Campbell's appointment would encourage more clergymen to learn Welsh. But alas Campbell's Welsh was not the pure Welsh of Morgan, and he hastily discarded it after his consecration as bishop of Bangor.[21]

****

All these issues and controversies were taking place against a more personal background which caused Morgan great despair and anguish, and clearly added to the bitterness he felt against Bishop Short and probably caused his paranoia about him. It concerned the illegitimate son of Morgan's maid, Elizabeth

Williams. In the summer of 1852 she was dismissed from his service, and went to the north of England, lodging with a Roman Catholic family. In early December she gave birth to this son, but she died from typhus fever at the end of the month. The incumbent of that district obtained for Morgan a surgeon's certificate, which indicated that the child was not premature, and that the pregnancy had gone the usual period of 40 weeks. The child would have been conceived, therefore, while Morgan was absent 'on a tour' from Tregynon during February and March of that year. In March a long and bitter correspondence commenced with Short when Morgan wrote to the bishop requesting that he might resign the curacy of Mochdre and have leave of absence from Tregynon. The correspondence continued with the bishop's accusation that Morgan was the father of this child on the grounds that the family with whom his former maid lodged had said so and that he had provided money for her necessities (which he denied) and paid her funeral expenses. Furthermore, the bishop accused Morgan of trying to swear the child on another man, adding that 'the evidence is of that character that it can leave no one in doubt on the mind of anyone who reads it'. However, by May the bishop seemed convinced that the evidence against Morgan was insufficient to justify any charges being brought against him, and he was ready to receive Morgan's medical certificate for leave of absence and his nomination of an assistant curate to serve Tregynon. Both were accepted, and Morgan assumed the matter was at an end.

Some time later Morgan requested the bishop to countersign his letters testimonial, probably to enable him to obtain a curacy in another and healthier parish. Even though these letters testimonial had been signed by four beneficed clergymen of the diocese of St Asaph who were neighbours of Morgan and knew him intimately, all of whom, with the archdeacon and rural dean, would probably have formed a commission of enquiry had charges been preferred against Morgan, the bishop not only refused to countersign these letters testimonial but also declined to offer any reason for this refusal. This was in spite of Morgan's unqualified denial of these accusations, the withdrawal by the bishop's proctor of the 'offensive and revolting' charge that he had tried to persuade the woman to swear the child onto another man, and the warning by the minister of the district where she had lodged about the character of the people on whose evidence the bishop was relying. Though Morgan had left the matter in the bishop's hands, the bishop had done nothing to investigate the truth of these allegations, and now, claimed Morgan, he stood as both accuser, judge, jury and executioner. Requesting the bishop's retraction of the charges, Morgan felt bound to add that if he did not do so, he would have to commence legal proceedings. The bishop did not reply. Morgan's solicitor was requested to act. But he had to report that counsel had advised that 'he had no remedy at law or otherwise under the peculiar circumstances of the case'.

Writing to Archdeacon Clive of Montgomery, Morgan claimed that the bishop was well aware that he (Morgan) could not obtain any legal redress from him, and was sheltering behind legal technicalities. He vowed to continue fighting for justice, not only for himself, but for every parochial clergyman in the Church: 'I am the victim today: you or any one else may be to-morrow. No clergyman is safe, whatever his position, character, or service may be; he is liable to be totally ruined by accusations preferred in this manner from private motives, without even the pretence of proof or justification; nay, in the very face of the admission that there exists no proof or justification to ground such accusations upon. Such a precedent places the good name and livelihood of every clergyman at the mercy of the caprice or vindictiveness of any individual bishop.' Though Clive suggested he could establish his innocence by asking the minister of the district to reveal the confession the woman had made to him, Morgan declined, for the bishop had never asked him to supply any proofs of his innocence which, in fact, rested on quite different grounds. But the archdeacon too was misguided, claimed Morgan. He too took as 'facts' what were only 'assertions'. Furthermore, if Short was prepared to listen to the evidence of a confessional, he 'would soon prostrate the reputation of society at the feet of a Confessional Priesthood'. Instead, Morgan demanded 'the right of every Englishman to the law of his country, that his character should not be slandered away by Clergyman or Layman'.

During October 1854, while serving as curate of Romford, Morgan wrote to the archbishop of Canterbury. Making his usual attack against Short as an alien bishop who had surrendered his integrity in order to obtain a bishopric the duties of which he could not fulfil, Morgan stated that he himself was a 'staunch supporter of the right of the Welsh Church to Welsh-speaking and Welsh-preaching Bishops'. For this and other reasons, he had been selected by Dr Short 'from the commencement of his episcopate as the object of his unmitigated ill-will and hostility'. So little had he disguised his feelings that Short had been forced to apologise to his uncle, Sir David Davies, for comments made about Morgan. Unable to obtain redress from the law, he had left the diocese, but although his letters testimonial had been signed by beneficed clergymen in the diocese of St Asaph, and other testimonials counter-signed by three other bishops, Short had declined to countersign them. The result was that the bishop of Rochester was unable to licence him and he would be forced to leave his curacy. His character had been defamed and lied away, his professional livelihood destroyed, his fair and honourable prospects in the Church utterly ruined, 'by a man who takes advantage of his own infamous slander – a slander, for which, by his own confession, he neither had nor expected to obtain any evidence – to gratify his feelings of personal animosity', and who had cowardly refused to give any reasons for his disgraceful conduct. Could the archbishop intervene and offer him justice at last? The archbishop replied he had no such authority, and felt that he 'scarcely knew any one less likely to act unjustly towards a brother clergyman'. Archbishop Longley was a close friend of Bishop Short.

Consequently Morgan appealed to the Queen in Council, requesting the council to require Dr Short 'to be confronted face to face with your Petitioner, to substantiate or retract the accusations he has preferred' against him, or to adopt any other cause which might promote justice in his particular case. No answer was received, not even to a second application. Morgan now wrote to Lord John Russell, as premier, pointing out that he, Lord John, had placed 'the temporal prospects of the whole Clergy of St Asaph' at risk, for it was to be anticipated that those clergymen who were averse to Short's appointment because of his unfitness for the see (known to Lord John when he appointed him) and his 'unscrupulous' character, would be marked out 'as the special objects of his vindictiveness'. Lord John had himself argued that the Latin Mass was a 'mummery' but there was little difference between this and Short's case, save that for practising it he received a peerage, a palace, extensive patronage and a substantial revenue. Furthermore, the first requisite demanded of a missionary was that he should be master of the language spoken by his converts. Because Lord John was fully aware of the facts of Short's insufficiency for a Welsh see, Morgan claimed he was 'now answerable . . . for the inevitable results towards both the clergy and the laity of a flagrantly unfit and unconstitutional nomination'. Though he had every right to expect, under these circumstances, Lord John's assistance to enable him to obtain redress and reparation for the wrong which he was sustaining, in contempt of the whole spirit of the English law, Morgan regretted that his expectation was probably a delusion.

However, Morgan did receive an answer. His petition, Lord John wrote, did not fall under the jurisdiction of the Queen in Council unless it was brought before the Queen 'in the form of an appeal from one of the Ecclesiastical Courts'. Morgan, realising the cost of such a procedure would be in the region of a few thousand pounds, and feeling an even heightened sense of injustice, wrote in reply that having exhausted all other means of redress he would have to publicly post Dr Short 'as a most injurious and infamous calumniator' and to draw the eyes of every Englishman 'to the position in which a fellow-subject is placed by an act of Episcopal oppression, and to the deplorable defect in the law, made known by his Lordship's reply'.

In the same month, November 1854, Morgan ordered a thousand copies of a broadsheet to be printed. The circumstances of his case, the accusations made against him, and the impossibility of obtaining justice were specified in it, and the broadsheet ended with Morgan's statement that he 'does hereby protest, publish, and proclaim the said Dr Thomas Vowler Short, Bishop of St Asaph, as a most injurious and infamous calumniator' of his good name and character. This was circulated among the clergy of Short's diocese and in various other places. The circumstances of this case were published in a pamphlet, *Correspondence and Statement of Facts connected with [his] Case and [Bishop] Short of St Asaph*. The pamphlet contained some personal remarks about Short, namely that his rule was characterised by his hatred of all things Welsh, and ended with the promise that more would be written about these episcopal corruptions and the need for reform. This promise was fulfilled in the pamphlets already mentioned.[22]

As a result of this activity Short sequestrated Morgan's living, claiming that Morgan was not paying his curate the agreed rate. Morgan counter-claimed that as Short had prevented him retaining the curacy of Romford, he needed the money in order to support himself. Short now placed the living into the hands of Morgan's curate, Augustus Field, and ensured that all the income of the parish was paid to him. In the first few months of 1855 Short served a monition on Morgan ordering him to appear before him at his London home regarding this matter. Morgan did so, not for the purpose of obeying the mandate, but to repudiate it, on the grounds that he rejected any authority claimed by Short 'in his capacity of Bishop of St Asaph, in the British Church of the Principality of Wales'. This was because of his incapacity, as evidenced by the Scriptures, Liturgy, Homilies and laws ecclesiastical, to serve as an non-Welsh speaker in a Welsh diocese. Appealing to the archbishop once more, he was told that the archbishop had no power to enter into his case 'unless brought before him in due course of law'. Morgan now maintained that this was precisely what he was doing in disputing the legality of Short's appointment, under the terms of 1 & 2 Victoria c. 106 (presumably section 111, 'the mode of appealing to the archbishop of the Province'), and consequently asked what security he was to give to the archbishop for the payment of costs, as that statute required. His two applications met with no response, and a reply to his third indicated, briefly, that the case did not come under the authority of the statute Morgan had quoted. Although for a time Morgan believed that Short had abandoned the sequestration of his living now that public pressure had been bought against him, it was a false hope, for in June 1855 the process was repeated. The pamphlet in which all this appeared, in great detail, ended with another letter of Morgan's to the archbishop. He had attended the meeting of the Society for the Propagation of the Gospel in London, of which Short was a vice-president, and noted that he had left early. Had he not done so then he, Morgan, would have addressed that meeting and would have asked whether it was consistent for Short to be associated with an organisation whose principles towards the heathen were violated by himself in his own diocese. For every heathen converted by these missionaries, who were paid £100 per annum, the Anglo-Welsh bishops, paid at a rate of £4,000 to £5,000, lost seven Welsh people to Nonconformity. By God's help, Morgan concluded, he hoped 'to prevent the oldest

Church of this country . . . being treated by the Government and episcopate of England more ignominiously than the merest savages in the extremities of the earth'.[23]

It is easy to suggest that Morgan allowed his temper and perversity to defeat his common sense, but there is equally a sense of paranoia. His expressions against Short were ill-considered; archdeacons like his uncle had little to lose, but perpetual curates were in a different category. He was obstinate, refusing to produce the evidence he claimed would vindicate him, because it had not been requested or because the bishop acting on his own could not form a fair tribunal to judge his case. But the fact that four of his clerical colleagues were ready to sign his testimonials, and three other bishops to countersign them, is indicative that his innocence was believed in by those who knew him best. Short, although he did good work in the diocese, reformed its administration, and virtually re-founded its educational work, was clearly a sensitive man, widowed and childless, and perhaps in some respects was very similar in temperament to Morgan. It was a clash of personalities and, against the power and authority Short could command, Morgan had little chance of success. Yet Morgan's principal concern about the denial of justice was a valid point. So was his assertion that bishops in Wales needed to be Welsh-speaking at that time. Had he put the case in a more moderate and diplomatic style would he have been treated as he was, with a vengeance that was swift and ugly? But then had he been more moderately spoken he might never have been heard. Morgan was one of the first martyrs of Welsh nationalism.

The story does not end here. Augustus Field continued as stipendiary curate of Tregynon until 1863, Morgan having resigned his now long sequestrated benefice in October 1862.[24] With no income from it there was little point in remaining in an ecclesiastical limbo when Short refused to countersign his testimonials (though presumably he did so at a later date). Morgan's movements after 1855 are shrouded in obscurity. We know that in 1855 he was living near the Manchester area and in 1858 at Yeddington in Yorkshire, and that he served a number of curacies from the late 1860s onwards. In 1870 Morgan was curate of Marholm, near Peterborough, and, allegedly, in 1874 at Mapledurham in Oxfordshire. There were other curacies at Stapleton, Salop and Offord d'Archy in Huntingtonshire, and at one stage he appears to have formed his own 'church' at Broadstairs in Kent. There was two other flings at Short during 1856-7, one of which is recorded in yet another pamphlet, *The Letter of the Revd R. W. Morgan . . . on the Welsh Church to Lord Palmerston*.[25] Morgan had spoken on his now familiar theme at a public meeting at Rhosymedre. The curate of the parish, considering that he was 'out of love and charity with his brethren', declined to offer him the chalice at a subsequent communion service. Morgan claimed he had been excommunicated and, supported by the vicar and churchwardens of that parish, vehemently protested to Lord Palmerston and others. But the vicar's dismissal of his curate was vetoed by Short who described Morgan as a person 'circumscribed' in his diocese.[26] The other fling is Morgan's assumed participation in the so-called Mold petition. This, addressed to the House of Commons, sought the removal of Short from the see of St Asaph because of his linguistic incapacity to preside over a Welsh see.[27] Morgan died on the 22 August 1889.

Morgan, however, did not die simply as Richard Williams Morgan. He died under the title of Mar Pelagius I, Hierarch of Caerleon upon Usk and the British Patriarch of the Catholic Apostolic Church of the West, with jurisdiction over Britain and Western Europe. Morgan's hatred of England is said to be the reason why Caerleon was chosen for his see rather than the more orthodox Glastonbury. His actions here were very much part of the ecclesiastical underworld of the nineteenth century, when many Anglican clergy, feeling dissatisfied with their Orders, sought reordination at the hands of a bishop recognised by the Holy See, even though that bishop's orders might have been obtained by dubious and underhand methods. Such bishops were known as *episcopi vagantes* or wandering bishops, and one of their number was an unscrupulous adventure, Mar Julius (Jules Ferette), who claimed that he had been consecrated by the Patriarch of Antioch and had a special mission to establish an autocephalous Syrian Church in the West in the interests of the corporate reunion of the Churches. His claims have never been substantiated. He sold Morgan the idea of a Pan-Celtic union of Churches, consecrated him a bishop (while he was still curate of Marholm), and entrusted him with organising a new Church. Morgan's almost mystical and certainly romantic beliefs in the glories of the former Celtic Church, his dislike of Romanism, and his desire for a wider Christian society made him an easy convert, although he did little to forward his new position save to consecrate his successor.[28]

Morgan's life thus forms a small if eccentric episode in some of the vagaries of the history of the Church in Wales. It must have given him some consolation to receive a title far more resplendent than that of Dr Short, or even of the archbishop. Perhaps that was some compensation for his lost ambition and hurt pride.

ENDNOTES

G. H. Thomann has recently published a short biography of Richard Williams Morgan (Solna, Sweden, 2001). In it he reprints a number of his works, including his *Letter to Lord Palmerston* and his later liturgical work, *Altar Service of the British Church.*

1 R. S. Thomas, *Selected Prose* (Bridgend, 1986), pp. 138-44.

2 R. W. Morgan, *The Verities of the Church* (London, 1849), pp. 287 and iii.

3 D. G. Osborne-Jones, *Edward Richard of Ystradmeurig* (Carmarthen, 1934), pp. 60f, 66f, 72f. D. R. Thomas in his *History of the Diocese of St Asaph* (Oswestry, 1913), III 110, notes that Richard Morgan was vicar of Llanfor from 1816-19, having been previously curate in charge. His wife's name

was Anna Margaretta.

4   See O. W. Jones, "Tractarianism at Tregynon", *Province*, XIV (1983) 88. (He suggests that Morgan was 26 when he entered St David's College). Morgan's ordination after 18 month's study testifies to the soundness of his earlier schooling.

5   I. G. Jones (ed), *The Religious Census of 1851: A Calendar of the Returns relating to Wales* (Cardiff, 1981), II 32, 35.

6   *Correspondence and Statement of Facts connected with the Case of the Rev. R. W. Morgan and the Rt Rev Dr Thomas Vowler Short* (London, c 1855), pp. 3f.

7   The papers of Queen Anne's Bounty and Ecclesiastical Commission are housed at the Representative Body of the Church in Wales's Cardiff office. My article on the parish of Tregynon, utilising this material, appeared in *Montgomeryshire Collections*, 86 (1998) 115-22.

8   Jones, *Tractarians at Tregynon*; Morgan, *Verities*, pp. vi, 42, 61, 238, in particular. The quotation from Rowland Williams is found in his *A Sermon Preached at the Visitation of the Lord Bishop of St Davids at Cardigan, 1851, and A Sermon preached at St David's College Chapel, Lampeter* (London, 1851), p. 57n. O. W. Jones regarded Morgan as a Tractarian, a view adopted by Peter Freeman in a recent article in *Montgomeryshire Collections*, 98 (1999) 87-93. This is not the case. There was sympathy, but not the willingness to reinterpret the formulas of the Church of England in the light of Roman Catholic theology. Morgan's book, *The Verities of the Church*, amply illustrates this point. Nevertheless, Thomann in his biography (pp. 2, 5) suggests that in his later years, due to the influence of the Order for Corporate Reunion, Morgan adopted more "Puseyite" views.

9   R. W. Morgan, *Maynooth and St Asaph, or the Religious Policy of the Conservative Cabinet Considered* (London, 1845), quotation from pp. 3, 17, 25.

10   R. W. Morgan, *A Vindication of the Church of England in Reply to Viscount Fielding, on his recent Secession to the Church of Rome* (London, 1851), quotation on pp. 2, 62, 81, 97. Morgan also denied sacrificial priesthood and the doctrine of purgatory.

11   Many of his ideas probably came from his uncle, Archdeacon Williams, see his *Essays on Various Subjects* (London, 1858). Williams also wrote a book on Gomer. Peter Freeman in his *Montgomeryshire Collections* article (p. 87) gives no reference for his assertion that Morgan had the "termerity" to seek a Lambeth D.D. degree for his writings.

12   *Ecclesiastic*, 12 (1851) 344f.

13   Dillwyn Miles, *The Royal National Eisteddfod of Wales* (Swansea, 1978), pp. 55f. Gordon Sherrett in his *Illustrated History of Llangollen* (Llangollen, 2000), p. 130, writes that the eisteddfod was underfunded because none of the local dignitaries had been asked to preside at it; the Nonconformists were against it because its leaders were clergymen, and the clergy abstained from attending as they feared what might be said against the Anglo-Welsh episcopate.

14   John Williams, *On the Inexpediency, Folly and Sin of a 'Barbarian Episcopate' in a Christian Principality* (London, 1858). This was based on letters submitted by him under the pseudonym *Brawdol* in the *Carnarvon Herald*. The

quotations are from pp. 26, 35f.

15 Ibid, p. 58.

16 *Ecclesiastic*, 18 (1856) 1-13. This review was possibly written by Evan Lewis, later dean of Bangor. Writing to Dr Briscoe on 28 November 1855 (NLW, MS 7939B, fol. 78) Lewis hoped that his name would not be made known, lest "he should be made to suffer for his principles in calling in question the existing state of things."

17 This section is drawn from Peter Lord, *Words with Pictures* (Aberystwyth, 1995), pp. 147-50. The translations are by Peter Lord and used by his kind permission.

18 R. W. Morgan, *The Church and its Episcopal Corruptions in* Wales (London, nd), quotations from pp. 23, 59, 66, 72. Morgan by the use of statistics suggested that the Church had lost the majority of the population, but maintained that it was not a poor church.

19 R. W. Morgan, *Scheme for the Reconstruction of the Church Episcopate and its Patronage in Wales* (London, nd), quotation from pp. 30f. Morgan also wanted cathedrals to be reformed, for rural deans to be appointed by the clergy, and provision made for clergy widows and orphans. This scheme, he claimed, would prevent the bishops "palming their whole tribe" upon the Church, and depriving the Welsh clergy of the preferments to which they were entitled.

20 *Cardiff and Merthyr Guardian*, 1 November 1856, p. 7.

21 *Carnarvon and Denbigh Herald*, 28 May 1859, p. 6; 4 June 1859, p. 6. Morgan also complained about Ollivant's preferment of English speakers to dignitaries in Llandaff Cathedral, where no Welsh Sunday service had been performed for many years. An editorial in ibid, 4 June 1859, p. 4, criticised Morgan for his tone of exclusive leadership, but asserted that the appointment of any other than a native Welshman was an insult to the Welsh clergy.

22 Morgan, *Correspondence and Statement of Facts*, in passim, quotations from pp. 15-17, 24f.

23 *Correspondence between the Archbishop of Canterbury and the Rev. R. W. Morgan, in Appeal against the Legality of the Appointments and Jurisdiction of the Present Unqualified Bishops in North Wales* (London, 1855). Part of this appeared as an appendix to his *The Church and its Episcopal Corruptions in Wales* (London, 1855). Pp. 92-101. A letter in the National Library of Wales, Aberystwyth (Church in Wales Records, SA/LET/574), suggests that Morgan, who obtained his parochial income in two half yearly installments, had taken more than his fair share of them, and had only promised to make it good at the time of the next payments.

24 Church in Wales Records, SA/RES/140.

25 *The Letter of the Revd R. W. Morgan . . . on the Welsh Church to Lord Palmerston* (London, 1857). In this pamphlet Morgan continued his protested about Short's lack of Welsh and his apparent violation of the law. His and similar appointments had made the Church into a minority body of squires and officials. Those who argued that it was impossible to rectify the position as

163

such appointments were a matter of crown prerogative were wrong; Morgan had a statement from Lord Granville to this effect, while he also possessed Lord John Russell's statement that the Anglo-Welsh bishops were simply "Mummery Bishops". The policy of the English government to Wales was akin to that of Russia to Poland or Austria to Hungary. He hoped that Short would be translated to an English see at the first opportunity.

26 *Ibid,* especially pp. 9-20. The churchwardens argued that the bishop would have acted differently if any clergyman had been involved other than Morgan, "whose moral position is unblemished, but whose position towards yourself and other English bishops in Wales is well known."

27 *Carnarfon and Denbigh Herald,* 6 June 1857, p. 4, 27 June 1857, p. 6, 4 July 1857, pp. 4f, 25 July 1857, p. 5. One may suspect that Archdeacon Williams and Morgan had a hand in this petition, but an address to the bishop, signed by nearly all the diocesan clergy, expressing their support and loyalty, may indicate that the petition had little *public* support in the diocese (Church in Wales Records, SA/MISC/1723). The 27 June issue of the paper (p. 6) has a letter by Morgan which relates to this petition, although it is not specified. In it he claimed that Short was on the side of "Queen Mary's bishops of bloody memory", rather than of the Reformers, because he continued to perform their Popish practices and principles which were repugnant to the Word of God and contrary to the custom of the early Church. He hinted that if subscriptions were forthcoming a mandamus would be applied for in the Court of Queen's Bench in order to determine whether what was legal in the reign of Queen Elizabeth I was still legal in the reign of Queen Victoria.

28 P. F. Anson, *Bishops at Large* (London, 1964), pp. 43-7; R. T. Brandreth, *Episcopi Vagantes in the Anglican Church* (2nd ed, London, 1961), pp. 70, 78n.

David Parry: Y Gloch Arian

'So sweet was his voice and mellow his phrases' he was termed Y Gloch Arian, the Silver Bell, wrote J.V. Morgan of David Parry.[1] His reputation was as large as his physique was small.

Alfred George Edwards, the first archbishop of Wales, in his *Memories*, remembered to the end of his days a sermon he had heard Parry of Llywel, as he was then known, preach at Llandingat Church for a harvest-home service. Edwards was then a pupil at Llandovery College. 'His fame,' he wrote, 'was great throughout Wales.' He continued:

A short little man draped in a heavy black gown, he stood like a statue in the pulpit. There was no straining of the voice, scarcely a gesture beyond just the majesty of the hand. The Welsh was perfect, and there was a surpassing ease and grace of diction in the sentences so simple and yet so polished that flowed in a wonderful harmony.

'Unpreparedness' was the warning note of the sermon. The arguments with which he opened his discourse fell into their places naturally and spontaneously like well-disciplined regiments, and the whole movement seemed to reach its climax in a story which, with engrossing detail, enchained the hearers and illumined with a flash-light the moral of his sermon. A shipwrecked sailor reached his home on the Cardiganshire coast, and as he narrated to a crowd of relatives and friends the horror and the suddenness of the gale that wrecked his vessel, 'You must', exclaimed an awe-struck listener, 'have fallen at such a moment on your knees and sought God's help and pardon in prayer'. 'Oh, no,' said the sailor, 'we were too busy with the sails and the pumps to think of such things then.' More than sixty years have passed since then, and have not dimmed the impression of that service and sermon. Looking back over life and recalling the speakers I have heard from time to time, I still believe that Parry of Llywel was one of the greatest natural orators I ever heard. Trick or artifice had no place in his oratory; its effect was not only magnetic but magical.[2]

David Parry was born in 1794, in the parish of Llangan, Carmarthenshire. Both his parents, David and Dorothy, were staunch churchpeople and communicants, remaining loyal to the Church in spite of the Methodist movement then in its heyday. Parry was to say he owed all his early religious impressions to his mother who, noted for her piety, trained her son in spiritual paths and biblical teaching. From her, it is said, he gained his genuine piety and devotedness to the Church which distinguished him throughout his life. At an early age Parry experienced deep religious impressions, and resolved to enter the ministry of the Church.

As a result of this desire he appears to have been sent for a while to Ystrad Meurig School, but soon migrated to Carmarthen Grammar School. Before the opening of St David's College, Lampeter, this school was one of the licensed grammar or divinity schools at which men were trained for the Church's ministry. It was a seven year course, and at this school Parry spent his youth from the age of 15 to 23. There were many who argued later that these schools gave a far better grounding in divinity, and especially in pastoral theology, preaching and in the use of the Welsh language, than Lampeter ever did, and did so at less cost. During his time at Carmarthen the bishop of St David's was endeavouring to open his projected college at Lampeter, and the interest on some of the monies received was utilised for grants to such men as Parry, given on the basis of a competitive examination. He thus received the sum of £10 per annum, which must have been of some help to his parents who would have paid for his training out of their own slender resources. During the last two years of his course, Parry, with a few others, agreed to deliver to one another carefully prepared but extempore sermons, without the use of notes or manuscript, and it is said that all those who took part later became well-known as preachers. Their number included Grey Hughes, vicar of Newport and Mathry, William Leigh of Eglwysilan, Timothy Davies of Defynnog, and John Jones of Llansadwrn. Dr Thomas Walters, who quoted this illustration to a diocesan conference, regarded these men and some of their contemporaries as those who had 'raised the [preaching] standard of the Church in Wales when there was nothing but stagnation and apathy'.[3]

Ordained to the curacy of Crinon, a small Pembrokeshire parish, in 1818, Parry was preferred by the bishop of St David's, Thomas Burgess, to the parish of Llywel, in Breconshire, in 1821, and he was to remain here for over 40 years. In the parliamentary return of 1832 Parry stated that his was a parish of 1,800 people, and that his church was able to seat over half of this number. He also cared for a chapel of ease at Rhydybryw. Each church had a sermon each Sunday, while he catechised the school during the evening service. There was no glebe house in his parish, and he was forced to rent one for £20. It appears this was at Trecastle, outside his parish. Though his income amounted to £190 in tithes and an additional £2 in surplice fees, his outgoings included £32 in poor rates, £3 in land tax and £5 road tax, so his 'official' net income was £152. But from this sum the rent of his house and the upkeep of a horse needed for his visits to his scattered parishioners had to be deducted. However the position of Rhydybryw was rather uncertain. In theory it was a parochial chapelry, mainly in the right of having received some five augmentations from Queen Anne's Bounty of £200 each, which were used to purchase land in various Breconshire parishes and at Merthyr Tydfil. Their rentals produced an income for the incumbent of about £150 gross. But the incumbent was not Parry. Rather he was the curate of an absentee incumbent, receiving the sum of £60 per annum for taking the Sunday afternoon service and caring for the pastoral needs of the parishioners. The previous incumbent, a Mr Llewellyn, had died in 1831, having been appointed in 1791, and Parry wrote seeking advice from Queen Anne's Bounty as to his right of presentation as incumbent of the mother parish, the former presentation having been made, it seems, by the people of the parish. Thankfully, Dr Lushington, an eminent canon lawyer, ruled in favour of the incumbent as patron, and at the next vacancy in 1836 Parry appointed his brother-in-law, William Herbert, as incumbent, being unable to present himself by reason of being the patron of the living. As a result Parry was probably able to obtain a better arrangement for himself as curate. Herbert was also vicar of Llansaintfraed in Cardiganshire.

Parry appears to have served Llywel and its chapelry on his own, without the assistance of a curate, but in 1862 he accepted Bishop Thirlwall's offer of the parish of Defynnog, in the same rural deanery as Llywel. He was then 68 years of age, and in all probability this new parish was seen as a semi-retirement post, not because it was a small parish, for it was not, but rather because its income was sufficiently large to enable him to employ a curate to work part of the parish for him. At that time the incumbent was responsible for the stipend of his curates, and Parry could hardly have afforded to have employed one at Llywel on the income he received from it. Pensions were not available for retiring clergy until the end of the nineteenth century, unless they had private means at their disposal. Many had to remain in their parishes and see the good work they had done over the years collapse because of their inability to sustain it.

The new parish had an income from the tithe rental charge

of about £410, and a parsonage house. Nevertheless it was a strange parish to offer a man of his age, for it also included Ystradfellte, was spread over nearly 40,000 acres and had a population of nearly 2,500. In a letter of 6 January 1868 to the Ecclesiastical Commissioners Parry noted that the two churches were ten miles from each other and linked by a high mountainous and almost inaccessible road. He had a curate in Ystradfellte who also assisted in a neighbouring parish (where he lived), and another curate who looked after an outlying area. Part of the tithes of his parish belonged to the bishopric of Gloucester and Bristol, now administered by the commissioners, who undertook to act 'as a good landlord' in those parishes in which they held an interest. Parry requested therefore that the commissioners might offer him a grant for a curate in Defynnog, as he was unable to afford the cost himself, and either offer Ystradfellte an endowment of £100 per year, thus enabling it to become a separate parish, or to make up his own income to £300, if some of his existing income was surrendered in order to endow this new parish. The commissioners replied that the chapter had leased its interests in these tithes to Sir William Clayton, Bart, whose son, Richard Rice Clayton, aged 75, was the last life in the lease, and they would have to defer the consideration of any local claim until the lease had expired. It appears that Mr Clayton did not die until 1879, but the new parish of Ystradfellte was created in 1875; Parry voluntarily surrendering to the new incumbent tithe income valued at £102 per annum. The commissioners were unable to augment Defynnog with an additional sum in lieu of this loss until 1880, and by this time Parry had vacated the living by death.[4]

Within his parishes Parry was regarded as a fine pastor. Lewis Price of Llandeilo, who was instrumental in collecting the funds which provided a Llywel Scholarship at Lampeter, recalled two of his expressions: 'If you take an interest in your parishioners they will take an interest in you,' and that people for whom they cared pastorally should also be the 'people of their comfort.' At a presentation to Parry after 30 years at Llywel, when he was described as 'a most faithful and laborious servant in the vineyard of his Lord and Master', he replied by saying that he could conscientiously declare that they had been the recipients of all his reading and meditations, and that he had never forgotten them in his daily prayers. Towards the end of his days it was written of him: 'The vicar is not a Preacher only, but a pastor also in the truest sense of the word. His visits to the sick are greatly appreciated – his manner is so friendly, his heart so full of sympathy, his exhortations so pointed, cheering, and encouraging. He has a kind word and a friendly greeting for all who know him, wherever and whenever he meets them – and his capacity is at all times that of a peacemaker, throwing oil on the troubled waters.'[5]

We have already heard the testimony of A. G. Edwards that Parry was one of the best-known Welsh preachers of his day. He was known as such throughout south Wales, making frequent preaching tours there, and he occasionally ventured into north Wales. Taking up this theme a newspaper correspondent thus wrote on the occasion of his appointment to Defynnog:

When the position and influence of the Church for good were at a very low ebb indeed in Wales, Mr Parry stood nobly forward as a faithful gospel preacher; and helped to advance the efficiency of the Church establishment, by elevating the tone and raising the standard of true evangelical preaching and earnest piety among the clergy. Time was when Mr Parry stood almost alone as an able and faithful preacher in the Church in South Wales.[6]

Another (possibly Thomas Walters) wrote:

Mr Parry is a preacher of the pure Evangelical school of

thought. He preaches both in Welsh and English, but Welsh is the medium of his greatest power. The rare melody and mellifluous cadences of this grand old language seem especially suited to the [per]suasive and highly sympathetic nature of the Vicar of Defynnog, on whose tongue it is simply irresistible, with its melting pathos and charming silvery flow. His manner is natural and unaffected in the highest degree, without being common-place; and so tender is his own heart, that his feelings often overflow into tears in the pulpit at the contemplation of pictures and sentiments which, in his discourses, he brings before his mind's eye . . .

His sermons, Walters pointed out (and as Edwards testified), reached the heart, rather than the intellect, especially by the use of illustrations, and they had all the more power because he spoke simply and naturally, without the 'artifices of rhetoric'. His sermons, though long, were never tedious, because his pleasing voice, 'musical and sonorous', fluency of speech, and frequent change of subject, kept the attention of his hearers for an hour and more. However, Parry was said to have a tendency to 'eat his words', that is, becoming a little unclear to his hearers. Yet it was also said that his reading of the liturgy, especially of the litany, enabled the old prayers to appear in a new light.[7]

Whenever Parry was due to preach, the crowds came. At the consecration of St David's Church, Merthyr Tydfil, in 1847, he preached at the Welsh evening service. It started at seven, but the crowds were pouring in at 5.30 pm, and not only was every seat taken but the aisles were crowded to excess with people standing. The sermon lasted for one and a half hours, and gave, it was recorded, 'universal satisfaction'. A story is told that at the opening of a church in Carmarthenshire, the bishop of St David's (probably Basil Jones), was due to preach in Welsh. Seeing Parry present, he went up to him and said in what was recorded as 'an unusually kind and complimentary way', 'I feel,

Mr Parry, that I shall be altogether out of place in that pulpit today: it is I should be sitting listening to you, and not you listening to me'. But, as was usual then with the 'big' preachers who frequently itinerated on preaching tours or were regarded as the special preachers for major events, one good sermon could suffice for many occasions. That Parry was no exception is shown in an anecdote told about him some years after his death. One of his best sermons was from a text in Habakkuk, 'O Lord, revive thy work'. David Owen, Brutus, the controversialist and Welsh Church writer, heard this sermon so often that although he did not know shorthand, he was able to take it down, and had it printed in his paper, *Y Haul*. Parry was mortified: 'Brutus, Brutus,' he is said to have exclaimed, 'You have done for me now. You have taken away the best plough I have in the furrow!'[8]

One of the most important of the organisations utilised by the evangelical Welsh clergy as a means of teaching, outreach, and encouragement to their younger brethren, was the clerical meeting. These meetings had been started in the 1800s at the suggestion of Bishop Burgess, but by the 1820s they had developed into a format which closely resembled the Methodist association meetings, and were completely in the hands of the evangelical clergy. Both Bishop Jenkinson of St David's and his successor Bishop Thirlwall spoke against them, the first disliking their use of extempore prayer, and the latter, with even more emphasis, regarding them as akin to Nonconformist preaching conventicles where the worship became secondary to the preaching and the rules of the Church were flagrantly violated. But both bishops were insensitive to the needs of the Welsh people and the value of these meetings, which often encouraged people to remain within the Church instead of joining Nonconformist bodies. These attacks caused these meetings some disruption for a number of years, but by the late 1840s there was a general revival of them particularly in south Wales, and one was even established at Llandaff Cathedral to the lukewarm protests of Bishop Copleston.

It is hardly surprising that Parry was one of the leaders of this movement. Held on a monthly basis, and circulating around the parishes, the clerical meetings (in spite of their name) were attended by vast numbers of lay people, churchpeople and Nonconformists alike, although during the course of the meetings the evangelical clergy held their own private consultations. Two sermons were preached on the first evening, and on the day itself there were normally three services, at which three sermons were preached in the morning and evening services, and two at the afternoon. Such an occasion required a large number of preachers, so that there was opportunity for the younger clergy to gain experience in preaching (and be apprised thereafter by their elder brethren) as well as to hear the more notable of the Welsh and English preachers of the day. Such a meeting took place at Llywel in June 1848, when a 'cold collation' was provided by the parishioners for the visitors. Later that year Parry preached twice at a clerical meeting held at Cadoxton-juxta-Neath, being described as 'the most eloquent Welsh preacher' of his day.[9]

There was still some opposition to these meetings, and this comes out in a letter David Parry wrote to David James, then of Kirkdale, Liverpool, but later rector of Panteg, in October 1849. The occasion of the letter was the episcopal vacancy in the diocese of Llandaff, and in particular Archdeacon John Williams's desire to become the new bishop. He and his friends were campaigning for his appointment, and in a letter to James the archdeacon wrote that 'Parry Bach' and all the evangelical clergy had confidence in him and, having pressed upon him the necessity of standing for the appointment, had addressed the prime minister on his behalf. But it seems Williams was a little too optimistic in the use of that word 'all', for some of the evangelical clergy, believing that Williams was opposed to these clerical meetings and had persuaded Bishop Thirlwall to put them down, argued that if he became a bishop he would become 'a great tyrant'. Consequently Parry wrote a letter to James in order to refute these ideas and hopefully obtain the support of the evangelical clergy for Williams's candidature. He wrote as follows:

> In reply to all this, I can undertake to say, that he now seems one of the best friends the Clerical Meetings have in this country. He has attended and preached at nearly all the meetings, that have been held in this neighbourhood, since his residence at Llandovery. He has been always ready, when necessary, to plead in their favor – And his presence and services have tended to place our Meetings on a higher footing in the Country – every cavil has subsided – In fact he has done the Evangelical Clergy already a vast amount of good. And my heartfelt wishes are, that he will be our new Bishop. For Breconshire will henceforth be united to Llandaff. As I am fully convinced, that he would act in a popular way – put the Church into a successful train [--] and be a friend to the zealous Clergy . . .
>
> It is a sad pity, if this opportunity be lost, by our not having a Welchman appointed – A man acquainted with the Language, the habits, and the peculiar character of the people – The Church will never thrive in Wales, until this object be attained. And we must have Bishops, that will countenance popular proceedings in the Church – ere the Church in Wales will ever become 'the Church of the people'.[10]

Williams was too much of a Tory of the old school for Lord John Russell to appoint him. Instead he choose Alfred Ollivant as the new bishop of Llandaff. Ollivant would have been known to most of the evangelical clergy as a former vice-principal of St David's College, Lampeter, where he had acquired some knowledge of the Welsh language.

As a leading member of the clerical meetings and as one

who advocated the need for Welsh speaking bishops (and thus an indigenous Church as opposed to an Anglo-Welsh establishment), Parry was possibly held in some degree of suspicion by that establishment. Nevertheless he was by no means a bigoted patriot. His evidence to the 1847 Committee of Inquiry into the State of Education in Wales indicates that he saw the need for the English language to be better taught in the schools, arguing that it was the language of business and commerce and noting that all the books written for the improvement of the mind were in English. Nor was he a bigoted churchman, if the evidence of that inquiry is anything to go by. For he suggested that while there needed to be Biblical and moral teaching in the schools, especially to eradicate what he described as the contemporary sins of unchasity, blasphemy, and lying, he felt it wrong to teach the Church Catechism to those children who were not from church families. Indeed, Parry made it clear that he preferred unsectarian schools to denominational ones. Such denominational schools, he argued, perpetuated 'all manner of jealousies, strifes and animosities' between people of different religious traditions, whereas unsectarian schools would hopefully promote union, harmony and love. Perhaps this was idealistic, but certainly the use made by some clergy of their church schools as a means of proselytising Nonconformists was bitterly resented and caused substantial friction within small communities.[11]

Though Parry might be accused of compromising with Nonconformity over the question of education, and of adopting Nonconformist methods in the clerical meetings, all agreed he was a staunch churchman. His feeling for his Church emerges in this extract from one of his sermons written at a time before Tractarian influences had destroyed the doctrinal harmony between Church and Nonconformity. In this sermon Parry stated:

[T]he Established Church in England [is] the grand

machinery raised by God in his providence for evangelising the people of this country. I admit with sorrow and regret that this machinery has been sadly out of repair in times gone by, but rather than God's work should fall and be at a standstill, other irregular machines were raised outside the pale of the Church for carrying on His own great work in the salvation of souls. Still the improvement which has already taken place, and which is still going on in the Church, is a sufficient proof to my mind that God has not abandoned our good old Church. I believe that, at some time, it is destined to answer more fully and completely the end of its mission in this land; and when that takes place, when the grand old machinery has been completely restored, repaired, and adapted for diffusing the blessings of the Gospel, and for carrying the lessons of Christianity to the hearts and homes of the people, then I do not think those lesser machineries will be any longer needed; but as they were quietly raised at first, one here and another there, as occasion required, so also will their use be hereafter be discontinued, not by force or violence, but by a quiet moral revolution in the Ecclesiastical polity of this country.[12]

It is not surprising, therefore, that Parry rejoiced at the progress of the Church. When laying the foundation stone of the new parish church at Ystradgynlais in 1859, he said he once remembered the poor clergyman with a large family who was allowed to struggle alone with his parochial difficulties, without any one extending a helping hand. But now it was quite different, for clergy were sustained by the cordial co-operation of the laity.[13]

A reminiscence of him by Lewis Lewis suggested that when men, presumably the younger clergymen, had not grasped 'the faith once delivered to the saints', he would ask them if they had accepted the three creeds, the thirty-nine articles, the Book of Common Prayer and the Holy Scriptures. But he seems to have felt that the younger clergy were a different breed from what they had been in the past. Writing to John Griffith, vicar of Merthyr Tydfil, and commiserating with him that his expression about the Welsh curates, 'the bullfrog clergy', had been taken out of context and misinterpreted, Parry went onto say that curates were becoming scarce and difficult to manage. But worse, the storm clouds were hovering over the Church. Had those in authority only listened to 'our suggestions' the Church would have been safe (the reference appears to be the growth of the Tractarian movement), but now Parry felt that the stability of the 'Reformed Protestant Church' was doomed, due to the lack of suitable reforms at the right time. But they would have to do their best and leave the matter in God's hands. Parry probably thought the same of disestablishment, then looming on the horizon.[14]

It was a source of considerable offence to the Welsh-speaking clergy of the Church that men such as Parry, leaders in their own right who had done much to revive the life of the Church, were never recognised by their bishops. The *Western Mail* in its obituary of Bishop Thirlwall castigated him for hoisting over their heads, to places of honour and emolument, men unknown to the Church and who had done little to deserve such honour. 'The heart of the Welsh Church grew sick' over this policy, its editor argued, for such men as Parry or Griffith of Llandeilo (another noted preacher), would have been honoured to have received at the hands of their diocesan some recognition 'of their eminent and long services in the cause of the Church'. John Griffith went further and argued that this was a deliberate policy for the hierarchy disliked the 'preaching clergy'. It was well known, Griffith argued, that Parry had kept the Church alive in south Wales for 20 years, but he went to his grave, so far as his bishop was concerned, 'unhonoured, unwept and unpreferred!'[15]

Was this true? Parry had been appointed a rural dean in 1849, at a time when that post was almost seen as a sinecure or as a mark of episcopal favour. In fact he was an active rural dean. Thomas Walters, vicar of Llansamlet, speaking to the St David's Diocesan Conference in 1889, castigated the rural deans of his day for never undertaking their official work: he had been for 15 years in his present parish and had yet to receive an official visit from one of the three rural deans under whom he had served. How unlike Parry, under whom he had served in Ystradgynlais. Parry made an inspection of every parish in the deanery before he filled up certain returns.[16]

Those who made those allegations were possibly thinking of Parry as being elevated to the position of canon, archdeacon, dean or even bishop. Lady Llanover, that great and vocal champion of the Welsh-speaking clergy, suggested Parry's name to Gladstone in 1870 as the prince of Welsh preachers, when he was anxious to obtain a Welsh-speaking preaching bishop for St Asaph in order to outflank and win back the Nonconformist population to the Church. Other names she suggested were David James of Panteg, John Griffiths of Neath and Griffiths of Llandeilo (who nearly obtained the appointment). Gladstone's eventual choice of Joshua Hughes of Llandovery was certainly not to her taste, although he was very much the sort of clergyman Gladstone had in mind. However, her ladyship rather spoilt the position for Parry by claiming he was 'too old'. But without a university background or the social elevation of a good marriage (which Hughes possessed), Parry would not have been considered in any case. Bishops, after all, even Welsh bishops at that time, were members of the House of Lords and had to mix with the aristocracy of the realm on equal terms.[17]

Such strictures were a little unjust on Thirlwall, although it may be argued that he was no judge of men. It may be that he was a little annoyed that Parry's name had been quoted by no less a paper than the London *Sun* as amongst those Welsh clergy who, for their learning, moral worth and piety, were qualified to be episcopal candidates for the vacancy Thirlwall himself was to fill. Most of the other names quoted were of men who were then, or who became, senior dignitaries within the Welsh Church, such as Dean Bruce Knight, Dean Lewellin, Archdeacon John Williams, Archdeacon Richard Newcombe, Archdeacon John Hughes of Llanbadarn, and William Jenkins Rees of Casgob. On the other hand the bishop may not have exactly appreciated Parry's connection with the clerical meetings, but Parry certainly did receive preferment from him in the office of rural dean.[18]

David Parry married the daughter of David Herbert, vicar of Llansantffraid and Llanrhystud in Cardiganshire in which latter parish the clerical meetings still survive albeit in a different shape. Herbert, with Bishop Burgess's blessing, had managed to prevent his congregations from flowing over into Methodism (Llangeitho being a neighbouring parish), by utilising Methodist activities within the Church's worship, such as congregational singing, an all age Sunday School, seiats and prayer meetings, and by encouraging lay participation in the work of the Church.[19] His influence must have had some effect on Parry's ministry and style.

David Parry died in 1877. He had lived up to the tribute paid to him in 1852: 'a Welsh orator, equalled by few, surpassed by none; a firm and unflinching supporter of the Established Church; of a sound Evangelical and Protestant principles; and a most faithful and laborious servant in the vineyard of his Lord and Master.' Twenty-five years after his death a Nonconformist preacher wrote of him, 'an excellent preacher, and always kind to me . . . Had the majority of the clergy been like him the Church of England would be crowded and Dissent at a discount.'[20] Judging Parry's concern for the reunion of the churches, this was a fine and just tribute to his memory. But regretfully the age of preaching, which he typified, was by that time in decline.

ENDNOTES

1   J. V. Morgan, *The Church in Wales in the Light of History* (London, 1918), p. 151.
2   A. G. Edwards, *Memories* (London, 1927), pp. 86f.
3   This, and other aspects of his life, are drawn from an article entitled "Portraits of Welsh Preachers" in *Weekly Mail*, 31 January 1874, p. 5: and *Report of the St David's Diocesan Conference*, 1882, p. 45.
4   The papers of the Ecclesiastical Commission and Queen Anne's Bounty. The EC papers also include the 1832 return. See also, I. G. Jones and D. Williams (eds), *The Religious Census of 1851: A Calendar of the Returns relating to Wales* (Cardiff, 1976), I 581 – the morning attendance is given as 300 plus 36 scholars, and evening 200 plus 90 scholars, and there were 80 free seats and 348 other, that is, rented, probably for church maintenance costs. Other details are to be found in T. W. Barker, *The Diocese of St David's: Particulars relating to the Endowment of Livings* (Carmarthen, 1907), IV 48f, and Theophilus Jones, *A History of the County of Brecknock* (Glanusk edn, Brecon, 1930), IV 104.
5   *Haul*, 1906, pp. 423f; *Cardiff and Merthyr Guardian* (CMG), 8 May 1852, p. 8; *Haul*, 1852, p. 203, and *Weekly Mail*, 31 January 1874, p. 5.
6   Quoted in *Weekly Mail*, 31 January 1874, p. 5.
7   *Weekly Mail*, 31 Jan 1874, p 5; *Haul*, 1846, p 296.
8   CMG, 11 September 1847, p. 3; *Weekly Mail*, 31 January 1874, p. 5, and *Cardiff Times*, 4 February 1888, p. 1.
9   Roger L. Brown, *The Welsh Evangelicals* (Cardiff, 1986), pp. 58-65; CMG, 17 June 1848, p. 3, and 18 November 1848, p. 2.
10 National Library of Wales, Aberystwyth, *Letters from Llanbadarnfawr Parish Chest*, typescript, pp. 29-31. The Commissioners wished to revise diocesan boundaries; one scheme, then contemplated, was to add the archdeaconry of Brecon to the diocese of Llandaff.
11 *Report of the Commissioners of Inquiry into the State of Education in Wales* (London, 1848), pp. 232, 312f, 355f.
12 *Weekly Mail*, 31 January 1874, p. 5.
13 CMG, 23 July 1859, p. 6.
14 *Western Mail*, 23 Feb 1897, p. 7; South Glamorgan Library, Cardiff, MS 3510, fol. 12, letter of Parry to Griffith, 10 January 1870. Parry also supported Griffith is his protest about the anti-Church stance of the Welsh language and Nonconformist periodical *Cymro*, which was "calculated to do infinite mischief": CMG, 27 December 1851, p. 3.
15 *Western Mail*, 29 July 1875, p. 6, and John Griffith, writing in *The Red Dragon*, 2 (1882) 7.
16 *Report of the St David's Diocesan Conference*, 1889, p. 31.
17 British Library, Gladstone MSS, Addit MS 44423 fol. 169 and 44425, fol. 25, letters of Lady Llanover to Gladstone, dated 17 November 1869 and 19 February 1870.
18 *Carnarvon and Denbigh Herald*, 25 July 1840, quoting the *Sun*.

19 David Evans, *Atgofion* (Lampeter, 1904), pp. 8f, 20, and Brown, *Welsh Evangelicals*, pp. 56f.
20 CMG, 8 May 1852, p. 8, and Thomas Lewis, *My Life's History* (Newport, 1902), p. 35.

The Nautical Vicar of Swansea
Edward Burnard Squire, Vicar of Swansea 1846-76

'The present Vicar is the Rev. E.B. Squire,' reported John Lewis in his 1851 *Swansea Guide*, adding that he ranked 'as one of the most active and energetic amongst the Evangelical Clergy'.[1] Squire's ministry of thirty years in Swansea has been eclipsed by those of his successors, especially Allan Smith and Talbot-Rice, but it was he who laid the foundation stones on which these men were able to build.

A Devon man, Squire was the son of William Squire, described as 'Esquire', of Sidmouth, but probably living in reduced circumstances, as his son, at the age of 14 in 1818, entered the service of the East India Company, presumably as a naval cadet. Gazetted a lieutenant in the Indian navy in 1824, he commanded the sloops *Mercury* and *Thetis* in the First Burmese War of 1826, was appointed flag lieutenant to Commodore Sir John Hayes, and was present at the capture of Rangoon. Two years later, changing directions, he was appointed as a captain in the Indian Army. His naval training and manners remained with him to the end of his life. As his obituary in the *Cambrian* suggested, he retained the manners of the quarter deck throughout his ministry, with his strict discipline, gruffness in manner and speech which often repelled although it hid a genial and kind man. The natural tenderness of the man was hidden under the sternness of the officer. His piercing eye in a weather beaten face, and his leaning forward in his walk, also mentioned, equally spoke of his naval experience. Nor did Squire forget his days in India, for one of his published sermons was sub-titled *The British Sovereignty in India*. Preached in 1846, he chastised the East India Company for taking idolatry under its patronage and for refusing to allow missionaries to enter its jurisdiction. But he saw the providence of God in allowing England to obtain the sovereignty of India.

After some years in the Bengal Pilot Service, Squire changed direction again during the 1830s, and was appointed lay agent of the Church Missionary Society at Singapore, where he helped found the Singapore Bible Association. Between 1836-40 he was the Church Missionary Society's agent at Walan Archipelego in China, but on the commencement of the Opium War he was expelled from that country. Returning to England, Squire entered St Bees Theological College in Cumberland, which specialised in preparing non-graduates for ordination. After ordination Squire served curacies in Lancashire and at Burslem in the Potteries before being appointed vicar of Swansea in 1846 by its patron, the evangelical Church Patronage Society. This society had purchased the patronage from the Morris family some years earlier, in order to further its aim of establishing centres of evangelical churchmanship and influence throughout England and Wales. Squire's predecessor, Shirley Bunbury, had been the Society's first appointment to Swansea, but he had died tragically young after a short ministry, some suggesting that his death was a result of over-emotion generated by his controversy with a local Unitarian minister, George Browne Brock.[2]

When Squire came to Swansea, he realised that the Church there was almost spiritually destitute. Bunbury had been able to achieve little, and his predecessor, the redoubtable Dr Hewson, had occupied the living for many years but had served it more to his own advantage than for the benefit of his parishioners. Schools had to be provided, church planting encouraged, the laity mobilised for Church and Christian work, and the Gospel proclaimed. The parish had a population of 30,000, and at a time when the approved norm was one clergyman for every

2,000 people, Squire had to manage with one curate and a lay assistant, both financed by the Church Pastoral-Aid Society. When he had first requested a grant, Squire was told that the Society's finances were exhausted, but a benevolent lady had offered a curate's stipend to the most distressing case on its books, and his application was unanimously selected. At a later date Squire wrote that even though he had laboured as a missionary in a foreign land he had never been called upon to such exertion of means and strength as he was now required to give. Indeed, his parish was one of those places which had brought to light a spiritual destitution which people had never dreamed could exist in our 'highly favoured land'.[3] But such was his success that A.M. Christopher, rector of St Aldates Church in Oxford (where he had a major evangelical ministry to the University), described Squire to a meeting of the Church Congress as an example of the benefit of ordaining non-university men who had previously worked in secular occupations.[4]

One of Squire's first tasks was to divide his vast parish into districts of roughly 40 houses each. He then persuaded members of his congregation to accept responsibility for a district. His aim was that every house should be visited weekly, and to this end he obtained vast supplies of tracts. These he kept in bundles, so that when one district was completed, the bundle would be passed on to the next. The work was later formalised into the Parochial Visiting Association. The visitors, who met monthly for prayer, not only read the Scriptures and prayed in 'their' homes, but also invited the wives to Mothers' Meetings, commended the clothing clubs run by the parish, and distributed relief where needed 'with words of kindly advice and sympathy as well as by acts and deeds'. It is said that the parish relieved over 2,000 people each year. Within two years of his arrival, Squire was able to report that he, his curates, and a Scripture reader, had paid 3,200 visits to the sick, ignorant and afflicted, while 2,800 people had gathered together in various cottage meetings to hear the Word of God 'read and expounded'. As Fred Cowley remarks, it was through this ministry that St Mary's Church lost its reputation of being a place of worship for the rich and respectable and developed instead a deep concern for the poor.

Equally, the parish lost its insularity and became mission oriented. It is hardly to be wondered at that Squire with his background of mission encouraged his people to have a world-vision of Christianity and to support the Church's missionary activities. The 1866 *Parish Report* mentions the support given by the parish to the Church Pastoral-Aid Society, Church Missionary Society, Irish Church Missions, the Society for Promoting Christianity amongst the Jews, and the Missions to Seamen, as well as to diocesan societies. A number of these societies had local auxiliaries attached to the parish or to the town. By 1875 it was reported that since 1846 over £100,000 had been raised in the parish for the provision of schools, local concerns and missionary objects.[5]

There can be little doubt that Squire regarded the provision of schools as part of the Church's mission. Many thought that in this work lay his real significance, for when he first arrived at Swansea there was only one public school in the town, that at York Place, apart from the grammar and the dame's schools. The National School at Oxford Street was erected in 1848, and within a week 400 children had enrolled as pupils, even though they had to pay school-pence. It soon became a model school. Other church schools were established at Cockett in 1858, Oystermouth Road in 1862, and two years later St Helens Infants, while a ragged school for poor children was opened at Powell Street in 1862. In addition Squire's active encouragement led to the opening of a Pestalozzian school in Rutland Street. The Church Catechism would have been taught in these schools, and the scholars of the Oxford Street Schools were required to attend morning service at St Mary's, marching in procession from the school. Though many children from

Nonconformist homes attended the schools, Squire could write 'I do not remember *any* objection made by the Parents to the Principles on which they are based', though it must be admitted that he modified the catechism in order to suit the needs of Nonconformist children. In addition an Industrial Female Orphan Home was established for 45 girls, who were trained in the fear and love of the Lord in order to serve as domestic servants. To finance this educational work, described by Squire as training 'immortal souls for an endless eternity', £1,400 per annum was required in 1866, and this Squire obtained, wrote E.G. Williams, by 'dining and dunning' his leading parishioners. In all about 18,000 children were educated in these schools during his lifetime, and by 1904 34,959 children had passed through the Oxford Street Schools. It was an immense achievement, and as early as 1861 John Griffiths, rector of Neath, wrote to Bishop Thirlwall describing Squire's educational work as 'eminently successful'.[6]

If Squire regarded this pastoral work and his educational activity as part of the mission work of the parish, he also held from time to time specific evangelistic missions. In this he was a pioneer, for such missions were quite new in his day. Robert Aitkin and his two sons came on two occasions, in 1870 and 1874. During the first mission 40 sermons were delivered at St Mary's and 20 prayer meetings held, while drawing room meetings were arranged for the more well-to-do parishioners. The prayer meetings were held in the Oxford Street Schools, which could accommodate over 2,000 people, and these meetings were frequently carried on until midnight as the number of penitents was considerable. At the same time meetings were held for sailors and at the gaol, at which 17 prisoners were converted. It was a time for shaking the dry bones and establishing the believers, Squire wrote later, though he noted that the missioners were surprised at the littleness of the opposition encounted and the high proportion of the higher classes amongst the inquirers. Although seen 'as a little bit ultra-English', hundreds were converted, and these people formed the backbone of much of the subsequent Christian life of the parish. Another result of the mission was the starting of two prayer meetings which were held weekly in a room seating 500 people, one of which was held after the Sunday evening service. A rota of six laymen and seven clergy helped conduct these meetings. The only note of disquiet came from E.E. Rowse, who felt that had the Nonconformist ministers joined in and supplemented the work, even greater blessing might have resulted. The 1874 mission made use of the Music Hall as a neutral venue, and resulted in the building of a Mission Memorial Hall.[7]

This work of mission, and especially the development of schools and Sunday Schools, was a necessary preliminary to the work of church expansion. The accommodation provided by St Mary's Church was totally inadequate for the needs of the parish. The building of St Paul's Church, Sketty, by the Vivian family, provided some relief, and is a reminder that the parish extended to that distant part of Swansea, as it did to the Cockett area, where a lay assistant, funded by the CPAS, started holding services in homes and later at the school-room. He was replaced by a Welsh-speaking curate who was greeted with much apprehension by some of the inhabitants who had never met a clergyman before. St Peter's Church, Cockett, was built in 1856. Christ Church, serving the Sandfields area, was opened in 1863, consolidating a work which had started in a schoolroom. In fact these school-rooms were built with this dual purpose in mind, and formed a cheap and acceptable way of church planting.

At the hamlet of St Thomas, on the other side of the river, a curate was appointed to minister at yet another school-room, which served as the place of worship until a church was built in 1876. In addition mission chapels were provided at Swan Street (the Mission Memorial Chapel) and in the Greenhill area, which was predominantly Irish in character. A Welsh mission to the town resulted in the former church of St John's being reopened as a place of worship for Welsh-speaking churchpeople, but plans to establish churches at Greenhill and Waun Wen were suspended because of the ill-health of Squire's latter years, and his successor but one eventually carried out this work. Most of these churches became parish churches in the course of time, with one surprising exception. This was St James' Church, built to accommodate the growing middle class suburb of Ffyonne and Walter's Road. Although plans were laid in 1862, the church was not consecrated until 1867, and it took all Squire's powers of persistence to bring about the completion of this project. By March 1866 the building was roofed and glazed, but no further work could be done as the organising committee ran out of funds. Another £3,500 was required, but the Ecclesiastical Commissioners, overseeing the work, refused the committee's request that they as individual members of the committee should lend this money and reimburse themselves by imposing pew rents. Nevertheless pew rents were introduced, possibly as a means of paying off these debts. These financial difficulties probably made it difficult to provide an endowment for the stipend of an incumbent, and without such a stipend a parish could not be created. St James' church hall was built as a memorial to Squire's ministry in the parish.[8]

By 1876 Squire could record that the parish of Swansea possessed 8 places of worship, 6 curates, 2 Scripture readers, 40 district visitors, one Bible woman, 5 schools with 14,000 children within them, 5 cottage lectures and 2 prayer meetings. But E.G. Williams, then prison chaplain, considered that Squire's working of the parish was misguided. Instead of running it himself with a large staff of curates, Williams felt it would have been better had the districts been allowed to become separate parishes with their own incumbents.[9] It is a valid point.

It has been noted already that the accommodation at St Mary's Church was not sufficient for the needs of the parish, but even worse, much of that accommodation was in private hands and not available to parishioners. This was because of two factors, namely the existence of the rented pews, and the fact that whole sections of the church were claimed by two individuals as their private property. It is probable that these pew rents, which allowed individuals the exclusive use of a pew for the payment of an annual fee, had been introduced some years previously to Squire's arrival in the parish as a means of phasing out the compulsory church rate. This rate, paid by householders and used for the maintenance of the church fabric and the costs of its worship, was bitterly resented and being increasingly challenged by the Nonconformist lobby. Within his first year in the parish Squire made it clear at a vestry meeting that he had no wish to impose a compulsory church rate, and as a result he was loudly applauded by the Nonconformists present at the meeting. As parishioners they were entitled to attend it.

However, the real purpose of this meeting was not to levy a rate, as these people had supposed, but rather to equalise the pew rents in the central aisle of the church. Some pews, in the best position, were charged at 4s.6d. per sitting, but others, in less convenient places, cost much more. The meeting agreed to charge 10s. a sitting in that aisle, and ordered that the monies arising from these rents should be used for the care of the fabric and the maintenance of the worship.[10]

The other matter of vested interests may best be described in Squire's own words which he added to his return for the 1851 census of church attendance. He wrote as follows:

Space:	free 418, 212 being for children; other 953
Present:	morn. 743 + 101 scholars; even. 596
Average (12 months):	morn. 950 + 100 scholars; even. 800
Remarks:	Of these 953 'other sittings' in this Church the whole of the North Aisle which contains 120 sittings is *claimed by*

> *one individual.* The North Gallery containing 150 sittings is private property. The Chancel containing 150 sittings is the property of the Lay Rector. So that out of 953 sittings 424 are not under the control of the Church-wardens and those parts of the Church are comparatively empty while many of the Parishioners are applicants for sittings in vain.[11]

The lay rector was Sir Robert Morris. Although he had sold the advowson into evangelical hands. Morris had retained his rights within the parish church. The 'one individual' was Calvert Richard Jones, a local landowner who owed much property in Swansea, and who is now celebrated as one of the pioneers of photography. Ordained in 1829, he had briefly served as rector of Loughor, but on his father's death in 1848 he came to reside at the family home at Heathfield, Swansea. It is not known how his family came to possess these rights, but they clung to them with great tenacity.

Squire could do little but accept the situation. In 1869 it exploded. The previous year Squire's friend, and one of his most faithful supporters in the parish, Dr Edward Howell, died, and Squire preached a memorial sermon for him, which was later published. Mrs Howell desired to place a tablet to his memory adjacent to the seat he occupied in the church, and a tablet was thus placed in the north aisle. Almost immediately a furious letter came from Calvert Jones, then residing at 12 Lansdowne Crescent, Bath. The tablet had been erected without his consent and was in violation of his right as owner of the north aisle. Unless it was removed and the area made good he would take proceedings.

Squire in his reply expressed surprise that Jones's rights extended this far. It was the first time in 23 years that Jones had written of or spoken to him about these 'rights', and he regretted that they had now been brought to his notice in very discourteous terms. Noting that Jones charged people sitting in that aisle three times more than the charges imposed by the churchwardens in the corresponding south aisle, Squire calculated that Jones' income from these seats was at least 60 guineas per year. Thus over the years of Squire's incumbency Jones' income from this source alone must have totalled 1,000 guineas at least. For this sum, Squire continued, he contributed nothing towards the expenses of the services, the support of the clergy, or the maintenance of the choir and organ, and yet without these services his aisle would be utterly worthless. Calbert Jones and the lay rector both received hundreds of pounds of church revenue without having to contribute a penny towards church expenses, nor did they assist the work of the church schools, though hundreds of children living on Jones's estate in the town, now built over, attended them. Ownership of property entailed certain responsibilities, Squire pointed out, before making specific reference to Jones's ownership of the mortuary or Herbert Chapel. This had been utterly ruined by neglect, and when a relative of his had been buried there three years ago rain had poured on their heads through the roof of the building. Its condition was deeply resented by the parishioners, but unless the church authorities were as eager as he, Jones, was to enter upon legal proceedings, it would be hopeless to obtain a remedy.

In his parish, Squire continued, with 20,000 inhabitants, there were only 200 sittings for the labouring classes in their own parish church, but there were 386 sittings claimed by two individuals for their exclusive and pecuniary advantage. Their insistence upon their rights laid heavy burdens on others, and in particular had led to the exclusion of the poor 'and him that hath no helper' from their own parish church, and this position in turn had manifestly encouraged and perpetuated dissent. It was sad to see the poor man's rights in his parish church lost through the neglect of the law and the rapacity of the covetous, and claimed by the rich man as his inheritance. And it was equally sad that Jones should threaten legal proceedings against a defenceless widow. There was something cruel about the whole transaction.

The result was that Mrs Howell was forced to move her monument; and Calvert Jones received the condemnation of the press; the *Western Mail* in an editorial even suggesting that a wall should be built to block off the north aisle from the rest of the church. The editorial continued: 'Odium is reserved for . . . one who stands foremost among the most earnest and indefatigable workers in the field of parochial labour, and who has done, in the face of the most trying and discouraging influences, vastly more for the Church in Swansea than can ever be known or ever be adequately appreciated.'[12] But there was no real redress, and the position continued, in part, until the 1920s. [13] Some alleviation might have come with a projected re-ordering of the church in 1875, when it was proposed that a new pulpit and reading desk be provided, the chancel galleries removed, and the nave, south and north aisles and chancel repewed. One assumes that by this time Calvert Jones and his family had surrendered their rights, and that some accommodation had been entered into with the Morris family, although they had created sufficient difficulties for the parish to obtain counsel's opinion.[14] The scheme had to be abandoned, partly because of a trade recession in the town, making it difficult to collect the promised subscriptions, but also because of some unpleasantness with Mr Pringle the organist, which divided the congregation (many of whom preferred congregational to 'cathedral style' music) and prevented the co-operation needed for the scheme to go ahead.[15] In addition Squire's death may have removed the driving force behind these proposals.

It might be expected that the incumbent of a parish as demanding and important as that of Swansea would have a stipend to match his responsibility. But this was not the case. In 1818 the value of the living was returned at £160 gross, made up of the vicar's portion of the tithes of £80 (the lay rector obtained £114 10s), glebe land at Cornelly worth £30 (probably derived from a QAB grant), and fees of £50. There were also gratuities at Easter, said to be between £10 and £80 per annum, but as there was no parsonage house a residence had to be rented out of this income. It is hardly surprising that Squire soon discovered that the income of the benefice was totally inadequate for his needs. Asking for assistance from one of the funds administered by Queen Anne's Bounty, he pointed out that while the *Clergy List* gave the value of the benefice as £291, his actual income was less than half that sum, namely £135, for the rent of a vicarage house and the voluntary offerings he was required to give had to be met from his gross income. The latter probably included a fair share of his curates' stipends for which he was legally responsible. Alas, the Bounty governors declined to assist him as his official income was over £200 per annum.

A further enquiry of 1851 returned Squire's net income at £217. However, the governors declined to allow any of his 'voluntary' contributions to be included as deductions against his income. The tithe rent charge produced £100, although it had been commuted at £142, surplice fees came to £89 (though Squire maintained these had much diminished in recent years due to the opening up of other cemeteries and the civil registration of marriages), and the Cornelly rent together with interest arising on monies held by the Bounty made up the remainder. As the years progressed the financial position eased. In 1864 the living received a grant of £37 from the Ecclesiastical Commissioners, probably given to make up its gross income to £300 in accordance with its stated policy. In the same year the Cornelly glebe was sold. Comprising parcels of land known as 'Landgrove, Here Croes and Ddwy Erw fain', it also included a public house known as the Old House. Christopher Talbot of Margam was the purchaser, giving £1,800 for the whole property which was considerably more than it was thought to be worth. This money, with other smaller sums, was placed with the Bounty governors, and produced an annual sum of £65 9s. Kempe's Charity gave £1,350 in annuities to the parish in the following year, permitting a further income of £41 per annum. When St James' Church was built the income was increased by its pew rents, a portion of which appears to have been received by the incumbent, together with an annual sum of £34 which was the interest arising from monies which had been given to form its now defunct endowment fund.[16]

If the position had changed for the better over the years, it was still precarious in 1857, when a major dispute took place between Squire, backed by his bishop, Connop Thirlwall of St Davids, and the Swansea Burial Board. The board had established a new cemetery at Danygraig, as the churchyard was unable to cope with any more burials. But the new cemetery had to be consecrated by the bishop, and Thirlwall refused to do so until the vicar and the clergy of the parish were provided with transport by the board for the five mile round trip from their residences to the cemetery. Matters were procrastinated as the Order in Council for the closure of St Mary's Churchyard was enforced, and the burial board declined to provide such transport or to allow it only for the clergy rather than for all ministers of religion. Lewis Ll. Dillwyn, MP, interfered, and made all sorts of erroneous statements in the House of Commons and to the press, allowing Squire to make a number of assertive points in his later reply. Not only was his stipend far lower than Dillwyn stated, the member for Swansea had neglected to pay his Easter dues to the churchwardens for many years. And if he assumed that members of the Church could not be buried in consecrated land within the parish, he was obviously forgetting the churchyard at Cockett, so close to his own residence! But bishops can wait, and this one did, until the matter was conceded by a compromise. This restricted funerals to certain times of the week (thus answering Thirlwall's other objection at the additional burden imposed on a busy vicar by this new and distant cemetery), but the suggestion that the vicar should have a fixed sum of £100 in lieu of fees was dropped. It may have been 'a storm in a teacup' but the matter received national and parliamentary attention. The cemetery was eventually consecrated in January 1858.[17]

The old vicarage was in Frog Street (behind St Mary's Church) but had been disused for many years, as the surrounding property had developed into one of the slum areas of the town. Squire was forced to obtain rented accommodation, and for a time lived at Mount Pleasant, but by 1851 he was residing at 3 Brunswick Place, St Helens Road. But this accommodation was costly and Squire, writing to Queen Anne's Bounty on 9 January 1851 maintained that a vicarage house was urgently required as the stipend was inadequate for the support of a clergyman, especially as he had to pay the cost of renting accommodation. Squire thus requested the governors to provide him with either an outright grant for building a new vicarage or a mortgage, the latter being secured on the income of his benefice. They replied that they were unable to assist with a grant as his official income was over £200, but they also accepted his contention that a net income of £135 was insufficient to enable him to take out a mortgage with annual repayments of £50. However, they noted that they held in trust for the benefice various sums of money arising from grants given to the parish by lot and which had not been invested in land but instead held at interest. They would allow £500 of this money to be used for building purposes (in the end it was £625). However as the use of these monies for this purpose would correspondingly decrease the income of the living, Squire proposed to find a further £800 from private subscriptions, and hoped that the Bounty governors would meet this benefaction with a grant. This money was thankfully found, an additional £50 was added by Bishop Thirlwall, and a

£200 grant was given by the governors to meet these benefactions. It is thought that a considerable amount of this subscription was given by J.H. Vivian as a means of compensating Squire for giving up his legal right to appoint the first incumbent of the new church which Vivian had built at Sketty and thus allowing Vivian to choose his own man. This right normally went to the incument of the mother church.

The one acre site of the new vicarage, at the top of Walters Road and on the site of the present Belgrave Court flats, was purchased for £300, and it was assumed that the house would cost an additional £800. In fact it cost £1,215 and an additional £150 was required for the boundary walls, stable, coach-house and other outbuildings. The work was completed by 1855. For that price a substantial Italian style house was erected with three principal rooms, six bedrooms and two dressing rooms, school rooms and servant's bedrooms. Where the additional monies came from is not known, but the assumption is that they came from Squire's own pocket, for the Ecclesiastical Commissioners declined to assist in this work for a reason never specified. Bernard Morris notes an advertisement seeking to let the premises in 1858, stating that the loss to the living caused by the operation of the Burial Acts had made the house too expensive to retain as a vicarage, but he suspects that this was a ploy in the battle between the Burial Board and the vicar of Swansea as mentioned earlier. Knowing the precariousness of the income available to Squire, and the possibility that he was having to pay off some substantial loans on this house, his claim may have been true, though one suspects that some of his parishioners took the hint and assisted him, for the house continued as a vicarage until the time of Talbot Rice's vicarate in 1902.[18]

Squire's ministry was an evangelical one, and he laid the foundations which made the parish, and the parishes eventually formed from it, into one of the major evangelical strongholds of the Church of England. A man of his own age, he feared the influence of Rome, asking in one sermon 'what communion has light with darkness?', while he believed that the British Empire had come about in the providence of God for the conversion of the heathen to Christianity. He saw the Irish famine as God's word of judgement against the superstitions and idolatry of Papal Ireland, but he equally pointed out that the cholera epidemic of 1849 was a word of warning from God about the morality of their own day. The desecration of the Sabbath, the awful state of drunkenness amongst the working classes, and the neglect of Holy Communion and Bible reading, private and family prayer, were all cited by Squire as reasons for God's controversy with England.[19]

Writing of his achievement, many years after his death, E.G. Williams described Squire's initial work in the parish as having to 'clean out the Aegean stables'. He recalled Squire's own remark that when he first came to the parish and realised what had to be done 'he almost sank into the Slough of Despond'. Yet his iron constitution, determined will, indomitable energy and resolute perseverance (to quote Williams' own words), combined with his practical Christian faith, rebuilt the Church in that town and made it a power in the diocese and an example frequently quoted of the Church's 'revival'. This was seen not only in the number of new churches and schools built, but in the changed lives of people who thereafter exercised a powerful and humanitarian ministry within the community. And this was done in spite of the fact that Squire was said to be no orator but a man with little eloquence, although his sermons were described as being clear in argument and good in substance. He saw the work of ministry as including a concern for the poor and unprivileged, while he was a pioneer of both the mission movement and also, in Wales at least, of using lay people to further the pastoral work of the Church. Swansea has much reason to be proud of its nautical vicar.[20]

1   John Lewis, *The Swansea Guide, 1851* (reprint, 1989), p.21.

2   *Cambrian*, 31 June 1846, p.3; 21 April 1876, p.5; *Church Pastoral-Aid Society; Abstract of Reports*, 1876, p.26; Nemo (F.B. Ashley), *Pen and Pencil Sketches* (London, 1889), p.99; W.C. Rogers, *A Pictorial History of Swansea* (Llandysul, 1981), pp.155f. Squire frequently spoke of India and the Far East, see, for example, *Cardiff and Merthyr Guardian* (CMG), 19 May, 1855, p.4. His obituary noted his Calvinistic beliefs, and added that though he was no orator his hearers were appreciative of the good substance and the clear arguments of his sermons.

3   *CPAS Abstract of Report*, 1848, pp.19f.

4   A.M. Christopher in *Report of the Stoke on Trent Church Congress*, 1875, p.423.

5   E.G. Williams, *Move On! Or Church Progress in Swansea . . . During the Last Fifty Years* (Swansea, 1889), p.16; *The Parish of Swansea, Abstract of Accounts*, 1866, in passim and especially pp.26f: F.G. Cowley in Glanmor Williams (ed), *Swansea: An Illustrated History* (Swansea, 1990), p.163; *Report of Stoke on Trent Church Conference*, p.423; *CPAS Abstract of Report*, 1848, p.20. Squire also served as gaol chaplain until the appointment of a permanent one, though he used his Welsh curate to minister to the Welsh-speaking prisoners (CMG, 29 January 1859, p.5), and as hospital chaplain, with a stipend of £20 per annum, although there was considerable controversy about his appointment on the part of the Nonconformist ministers: T.G. Davies, *Deeds not Words* (Cardiff, 1988), pp.61f.

6   Williams, *Move On!* Pp.16f: *Abstract of Accounts*, 1866, p.10 and in passim; *The National Schools, Oxford Street, 1848-1948* (Swansea, 1948); Cowley in *Swansea: An Illustrated City*, p.164. The letter of John Griffiths is quoted in Connop Thirlwall's *A Letter to J. Bowstead, Esq. concerning Education in South Wales* (London, 1861), pp.64f. Griffiths noted that Squire had found many difficulties in starting these schools, 'among others the estrangement of many of his own congregation from his schools, and their support for the British Schools in the Town'. Squire also endeavoured to have a clause inserted in the revised scheme for Swansea Grammar School in 1856. This was to the effect that religious education and prayers should be provided by the master according to the tenets of the Church of England, although allowing for the conscientious objections of Nonconformists: *Swansea Grammar School 1682-1932* – a special number of the school magazine, 1932, p.10.

7   A Layman (E.E. Rowse), *Weighted in the Balances: A Review of the late Ten Days Mission Held in Swansea* (Swansea, 1870); S.C. Morgan, *Special Missions* (London, 1873), pp.23f; W. Hay M.A. Aitkin, *Reminiscences of the Eleven Day Mission Held at Swansea* (London, 1874): Williams (*Move On!* p.27) noted another mission in 1873 held in a tent by a Mr Cleworth.

8   Williams, *Move On!* pp.18-20, 26f; David Walker, *The First Hundred Years: St James' Church, Swansea, 1867-1967*; the papers of QAB and the Ecclesiastical

Commission (EC) for the parish of Swansea held by the Representative Body of the Church in Wales.

9   *CPAS Abstract and Reports*, 1876, p.26; Williams, *Move On!* p.33.

10   *CMG*, 27 March 1847, p.3. Voluntary church rates were still levied in 1869: *Western Mail*, 3 July 1869, p.5.

11   I.G. Jones and David Williams (eds), *The Religious Census for 1851: A Calendar of the Returns relating to Wales*, (Cardiff, 1976), I 258

12   *Western Mail*, 3 July 1869, p.5, and 5 July 1869, p.2; *CMG*, 31 July 1869, p.8. Although W.C. Rogers (*Swansea*, p.156) suggests that as a result of this controversy Jones retired to live at Bath, a point accepted by Calvert Jones's biographers [I.M. Jones, 'Scientific Visions', *Transactions of the Honourable Society of Cymmrodorion*, 1990, p.141, and Buckman Rollin, *The Photographic Work of Calvert Richard Jones* (London, 1900), pp.17f], his letters to Squire indicate he was already living in Bath by this date.

13   These rights continued into recent times. In 1895 the faculty allowing the rebuilding of St Mary's Church specifically preserved the lay rector's right to his own pews and to his own porch in the north aisle, though he was required to contribute £200 to the cost of the chancel. Counsel's opinion of 1924 made it clear that these rights were reserved by the Welsh Church Act, the matter having arisen through Sir Robert Morris's annoyance that his seats had been used without his consent and the north porch turned into a vestry. Eventually Morris accepted the church's position, stating that he had no wish to take this dispute to its full legal extent as he realised it could be obnoxious to 'modern' public opinion: EC papers.

14   The opinion is in National Library of Wales, Church in Wales Records, SA/MISC/94. The wardens had obtained a faculty which also permitted them to place the chancel pews choirwise rather than transversely. Sir John objected, insisted these were his own property, and threatened legal proceedings. Counsel maintained that as lay rector he had no other claim but to the principal seat in the chancel, and certainly no right, whatever an agreement of 1825 maintained, to receive any rents from pews in the chancel.

15   EC papers. The choir had refused to allow congregational music to be sung, see *Cambrian*, 24 March 1876, p.8; 31 March 1876, p.3, and 23 June 1876, p.5.

16   The 1818 return is in the QAB papers. See also T.W. Barker, *Diocese of St David's: Particulars Relating to the Endowment of Churches and Livings* (Carmarthen 1907), I 197f. Sir John Morris asked the Ecclesiastical Commission in 1870 if it was prepared to purchase his share of the tithes, as due to extensive building developments their value had diminished and they had been divided into numerous small payments. It is hardly surprising that the commissioners declined his offer: EC papers.

17   Rogers, *Swansea*, p.156; *CMG*, 8 August 1857, p.8 and 19 September 1857, p.8; Dorothy M. Bayliffe and Joan N. Harding, *Starling Benson of Swansea*

(Cowbridge, 1996), pp. 135-48, provide a comprehensive account of this dispute.

18   QAB papers contain plans and letters; Bernard Morris, 'Belgrave Court and the Old Swansea Vicarage', *Minerva*, I (1993) 12-16; J. Pugsley, *Church Life in Swansea and Neighbourhood* (Swansea, 1915), p.2f, incorrectly suggests that J.H. Vivian gave the vicarage in return for the advowson of Sketty.

19   See the various printed sermons of Squire: *Darkness the Characteristic of Papal Rose* (1850), *Defence not Defiance, Sermon Preached to the Volunteers* (1860), *National Guilt the Cause of National Calamity* (1847), *Two Sermons . . . on the Day Appointed . . . for Public Prayer and Humiliation on Account of the Visitation of the Cholera* (1849). Surprisingly, Squire was prepared to officiate at a masonic service at St Mary's, see CMG, 26 July 1851, p.3.

20   Williams, *Move On!* p.5. By the time of his death Squire was rural dean of Swansea and a prebendary of St David's Cathedral. He married three times, his last wife being a daughter of Thomas Bowen of Johnston Hall, Pembrokeshire, and a sister of Bishop John Bowen of Sierra Leone. She was presented with a purse of £700 and a portrait of her husband when she left the parish after his death (*Cambrian*, 30 June 1876, p.5 and 7 July 1876, p.5). One son is mentioned in the 1866 *Parish Report* as residing at Chile, and another two, educated at Swansea Grammar School, were ordained.

Conclusion

The clergy depicted in this book were men who cared deeply about the Church's pastoral and preaching ministries. In all probability they related these two ministries to each other, for as one preached one also built up a congregation in the Christian faith and enabled its members to apply the word of God to their own lives. We might even say that these men were grounded in their parishes.

No clergyman could escape, however, the difficulties of the times. The Church in Wales was threatened with disestablishment and disendowment. Its privileges were in danger of being lost and its responsibilities to the whole nation lightly set aside. Welsh Nonconformity, especially after the great Swansea conference of the Liberation Society in 1862, had declaimed that an alien Church had no right to its endowments and privileges having conspicuously failed to care spiritually for the whole nation, or to have regard for the language of the majority of its inhabitants. Those who argued in this way saw the very existence of Nonconformity and its combined strength over against the Established Church in Wales as proof of their assertion.

Such people could point to Horace Mann's religious census of 1851 for their justification. The census found that the Church of England in Wales had 1,180 places of worship, a total accommodation for 610,734 people, and a total attendance on the census day, counting those present at every service, of 189,706. Correspondingly, Welsh Nonconformity had 2,700 places of worship, seating accommodation for 610,734 and a total attendance of 777,315.[1] The interpretation of these figures is notoriously complex, but it certainly illustrated the assertion made that Wales was the land of Nonconformity. What was not realised at the time was that possibly up to a third of the population had little or no religious affiliation, while it was Bevan who pointed out that the statistics for the Church in many parts of Wales were equal to, and sometimes surpassed, those for English dioceses.

Even before these figures had been produced, sending shock waves throughout the Church, a vigorous debate had developed in an attempt to identify the causes of the Church's decline and the rise of Nonconformity. While this was often done in an attempt to find a scapegoat, it was also done in the hope that if a cause could be identified, then measures could be introduced to remedy the situation.

By and large, this debate concentrated on two causes. The first was the existence of the Anglo-Welsh bishops. Until Gladstone's nomination of Joshua Hughes to the see of St Asaph in 1870, no native Welsh-speaking bishop had been appointed since 1702. It was argued that these men, unacquainted with the language and ethos of Wales, or the spiritual fervour of the Welsh people, had failed to give any effective lead to the Church or to nourish within its body the eighteenth-century revival. As a result of their inability to understand or even to support that revival, its converts eventually established their own Church, the Welsh Calvinistic Methodist Church. Furthermore, because of their nepotism, English-speaking clergy had been appointed to Welsh parishes. The result had been a bias against the Welsh language. This, of course, is the position of R. W. Morgan. In many respects it was an ill-tempered argument and conclusions were drawn from unsupportable evidence. There was enough truth in these assertions, however, to enable this thesis to be widely believed.

By contrast, others believed that the real problem in the Church was its poverty. The Church lacked the resources it required in order to fulfil its spiritual ministry to the nation.

This was an argument generally accepted by the Anglo-Welsh clergy, such as Bevan, who was a powerful advocate of it, but even he did not realise that Nonconformity was even poorer than the Church!

The one area generally neglected in this debate was that the Church as a legal institution, with vested rights and life interests, was unable to respond with any sense of urgency to the growing industrialisation of Wales. The large parishes of the upper regions of Glamorgan and Monmouthshire, exploited for their mineral wealth, drew in vast populations. The Church was singularly equipped to deal with this situation. E. T. Davies's statement that the reason why Rhymney Church was so successful in what was 'a Nonconformist area' was because the Church had planted itself there before Nonconformity had taken a hold is significant. A Nonconformist cause might be started in a private house, move into a schoolroom, and finally into a purpose-built chapel. It might be served by lay preachers and part time ministers before it could become a settled pastorate. Its members were utilised in its work of ministry as elders and deacons. It was almost self-sufficient. By contrast, the machinery of the Church was slow and unwieldy, complicated by historic rights, vested interests, and the requirement of a professional ministry. Nonconformity could be up and running long before the Church was able to make any impact in a community. Only towards the middle of the century did the Church find some ways and means to overcome this dilemma, using lay agents, mission halls and schoolrooms, and obtaining funding from home mission societies. But in most instances it was too late, and the people who had 'turned' chapel never returned to the Church.

A further difficulty for the Church was that it had to minister in both languages. It was a bilingual Church. By contrast a Nonconformist chapel, until the turn of the century, was able to concentrate on one language. As many clerics made clear at the time, a bilingual parish needed a double machinery in buildings and clergymen, thus requiring more financial resources. The situation also gave rise to the strong feeling that the English-speaking church people were being given preference over the Welsh-speakers.

If these arguments defined the cause and extent of the problems facing the Church, what remedies might be available? Once again, there is no one clear answer to this question.

It was constantly pointed out, especially by Bevan, that a church 'revival' had taken place. The use of this word 'revival' was an unfortunate one, and ridiculed by many Nonconformists, as it tended to suggest that the Church had had its own spiritual awakening similar to the revival of the eighteenth century or of 1859. By 'revival' Bevan meant that the Church had woken up to its responsibilities and put its house in order. Absentee and pluralist incumbents were a thing of the past, dilapidated churches had been rebuilt, churches had been built and parishes created in the new centres of population, and native Welsh-speaking bishops had been nominated by the prime minister, with the result that the Church was now an effective instrument for its mission to the whole nation and was able to take its responsibilities as the Established Church seriously. It was unfair to disestablish the Church and deprive it of its endowments when it was now doing its work, and needed all its resources to cope with the great increase in population which had taken place. Squire too gave the same argument, albeit in a different form. The best means of Church defence, he suggested, was the Church doing its duty parish by parish.

There were others who advanced this argument a stage further. The Church had 'revived': it had adopted into its life such Nonconformist practices as Bible and prayer meetings, cottage lectures, hymnology, and lay ministry. There was still a doctrinal harmony between Church and dissent. The reason for dissenting from the Church, namely its lack of spiritual life, was now a thing of the past. Consequently, churches should unite, especially as all realised that there was still a mission to be accomplished and a common foe to face. Apathy, secularism and liberalism would far better be fought together than separately. Walsham How, to an extent, but David Jones and Parry more convincingly, argued this way. Regretfully, Nonconformity was suspicious of the Church because of the growth within it of ritualism and 'Puseyism', which it assumed was leading the Church into a Romeward direction. The Church's inability to prevent these teachings and practices was a major factor in Nonconformity desiring the disestablishment of the whole Established Church.

Another answer argued that the Church in Wales should be an indigenous Church. This term was defined in many ways, from R. W. Morgan's desire for a separate Welsh province, to David's Jones's hope that the Church should emphasise its Welsh roots more strongly and give priority to the Welsh language. Unfortunately, Bishop Edwards of St Asaph, the Welsh Church's self-appointed leader in its fight against disestablishment, took another route. In his defence of the Church he declared an almost all-out war against Nonconformity, and stressed that the Welsh Church was merely four dioceses within the province of Canterbury. Thus, in order to call on the help of the wider Church in his campaign against disestablishment Edwards had to emphasise its links with England rather than stress its indigenous nature.

The Victorian period was no golden age for the Church in Wales. Individual clergymen faced much hardship, both mental and physical. Some used inherited wealth for the good of the Church, as did Bevan, but most were like Rice Morgan, who lived in genteel poverty. Yet each used their gifts and skills for the good of the Church, many of them far beyond what might be expected of them as parochial clergy. Bevan thus defended his Church though his numerous writings, as did David Jones, while William Evans, Rice Morgan and David Parry gained a national reputation as Church preachers. No doubt all had mixed motives. Rice Morgan's insecurity seems to have made him economical with the truth, though his preaching gifts were widely appreciated. This was even more true of R.W. Morgan, his disillusionment and bitterness forced him to a strange and perplexing direction. Yet all these men, and many others, gave their gifts to the building up of the Church as they saw it, and we are the inheritors of their labours.

ENDNOTE

1   Taken from C. Barber and L.J. Williams, *Modern South Wales* (Cardiff, 1986), pp. 12f.

INDEX